Seven Stories Press
New York

First English language edition

Originally published in Spanish by Era Naciente SRL under the title *Fidel para principantes*, 2006.

Seven Stories Press
140 Watts Street
New York, NY 10013
www.sevenstories.com

In Canada: Publishers Group Canada, 559 College Street, Suite 402, Toronto, ON M6G LA9
In the UK: Turnaround Publisher Services Ltd., Unit 3, Olympia Trading Estate, Coburg Road,Wood Green, London N22 6TZ
In Australia: Palgrave Macmillan, 15–19 Claremont Street, South Yarra, VIC 3141

College professors may order examination copies of Seven Stories Press titles for a free six-month trial period. To order, visit www.sevenstories.com/textbook or send a fax on school letterhead to (212) 226-1411.

Book design by Era Naciente SRL and John Thornton

Library of Congress Cataloging-in-Publication Data

Kohan, Néstor, 1967-
  [Fidel para principantes. English]
  Fidel : an illustrated biography of Fidel Castro / Nestor Kohan and Nahuel Scherma ; translated by Elise Buchman ; additional illustrations by Miracle Jones. -- 1st English language ed.
    p. cm.
  ISBN 978-1-58322-782-4 (pbk.)
  1. Castro, Fidel, 1926---Comic books, strips, etc. 2. Cuba--Politics and government--1959-1990--Comic books, strips, etc. 3. Cuba--Politics and government--1990---Comic books, strips, etc. 4. Heads of state--Cuba--Biography--Comic books, strips, etc. I. Scherma, Nahuel. II. Buchman, Elise. III. Title.
  F1788.22.C3K64 2010
  972.9106'4092--dc22
  [B]
                              2010002177

Printed in the United States of America

9 8 7 6 5 4 3 2 1

FIDEL

I dedicate my portion of this book to the fond memory of
Mario Roberto Santucho, and to all the people of the world
who keep the sacred fire of rebellion burning.

—N.K.

My acknowledgements:
To Néstor and to Juan Carlos... for the opportunity and
the confidence.
To Grandmother Conce and Uncle José.
To Grandmother Nélida and Uncle Ruben.

—N.S.

Cuba: David vs. Goliath

Is it possible to resist the most terrible force on Earth? Can a small, sparsely populated country stand up against a nuclear power? As Vietnam yesterday and Cuba today prove, resisting such a power is possible, legitimate, and viable. The rebellion has a future!

Although the United States today enjoys a world power greater than that of the Roman Empire at its height or that of the Nazis in the time of Hitler, resistance by the people has not disappeared. Since its beginning, the Cuban revolution has opposed the abusive control that this ruthless giant to the north and its elite industrial military exercises over the entire planet. For this reason, the Yankees and their great media monopolies of (mis)communication devote their lives to slandering Fidel Castro.

But who is Fidel? Why do they continue to talk about him?

Fidel Castro in his youth

Fidel Alejandro Castro Ruz is born in Cuba on August 13, 1926, at 2:00 a.m. His mother's name is Lina Ruz González; his father, Ángel María Bautista Castro Argiz, is a peasant from Galicia in Spain. Although of humble origins (he fights as a conscripted soldier in the war of 1895), Fidel's father manages to accumulate enough money to buy five properties. These properties include sixty-five horse farms, approximately 870 hectares, located near Birán in the eastern part of Cuba. He grows sugarcane and raises cattle. In addition, he leases an additional 10,000 hectares of lesser quality. This land is surrounded by large North American estates.

In this rural world, amidst animals and vegetation, the young Fidel Castro—third son of a second marriage—spends his childhood along with his brothers and sisters: Angela María, Ramón Eusebio, Raúl Modesto, Juana de la Caridad, Emma Concepción, and a sixth sister. Birán is not even a village, just a small cluster of houses.

Fidel's early education

The young Fidel attends many schools. First, on January 5, 1932, he enrolls in the Escuela Rural Mixta #15 in Birán. It has a tin roof and wooden walls. Later, he goes to Santiago de Cuba. While there, he lives with another family. At the start of 1935, he studies at the Colegio de los Hermanos de La Salle; he is a student there for almost four years. Later he attends the Colegio Dolores de la Compañia de Jesús. Finally, he goes to the Colegio de Belén, a

Jesuit school in Havana—one of the best schools in Cuba, where the sons of the upper classes and the aristocracy are enrolled.

> Even though they're reactionaries, the Jesuits taught me a sense of personal dignity and honor, as well as the spirit of courage, strength, and sacrifice. This ethic, along with Marxism, made it easier for me later to acquire the perspective of the Revolution.

In the Colegio de Belén—where he arrives at age sixteen—the young Fidel proves to be outstanding in sports, and he is named "jefe de los exploradores de la Habana" (Chief of the Havana Explorers). He graduates in 1945, at the end of World War II, and then enrolls in the university scarcely a year after President Grau takes control of the Cuban government.

Fidel as a rebellious student

The young Fidel has his first political experiences as part of a student rebellion, where he is introduced to revolutionary ideas of justice as well as to humanist values: dignity, honor, liberty, decorum, equality, self-esteem, and an innate opposition to all forms of humiliation, abuse, and domination. As with many other Latin American leaders, anti-imperialist ideals and the the University Reform Movement's rebellion against neocolonial society deeply mark Fidel from the beginning. His early ideology is born from this youthful fight for qualitative ethical values, as opposed to the hierarchal values of the class-oriented, racist, commercial society of neocolonial Cuba. Young Fidel acquires a disobedient, revolutionary consciousness not because he comes from a poor, exploited class of workers, but as part of an ethical rebellion against a capitalistic, neocolonial society and its injustices.

> Knowing history permits us to understand the struggle today. Those in power would have us believe that there's no connection with the past, but the heroism of those who came before gives us strength to continue fighting for justice.

> THE POSTMODERN VIEW OF HISTORY DOESN'T CONVINCE ANYONE.

Cultural anti-imperialism

In contrast to European modernism, modernism in Latin America mixes an artistic discourse of protest against the commercialism of daily life with a political discourse on culture, social renewal, and anti-imperialism. Latin American modernism rejects imperialism on economic grounds, but also for ethical and cultural reasons. The Cuban poet and revolutionary José Martí (1853–95) is one of the principal instigators of this movement, but is by no means the only one. Martí, along with the Nicaraguan poet Rubén Darío (1867–1916), José Ingenieros (1877–1925) in Argentina, José Vasconcelos (1882–1959) in Mexico, and José Enrique Rodó (1871–1917) in Uruguay strive to defend Latin American culture in the face of the United States' dominance, its cutthroat diplomacy, and its capitalist system. Fidel's generation is also influenced by the University Reform movement, which spreads modernist ideas across the continent through protests and discussions. The anti-imperialist idealism of the young Fidel comes from this entire cultural constellation, in which Martí is one of the brightest stars. It is with good reason that Fidel, in his book *History Will Absolve Me*, cites both José Martí and José Ingenieros.

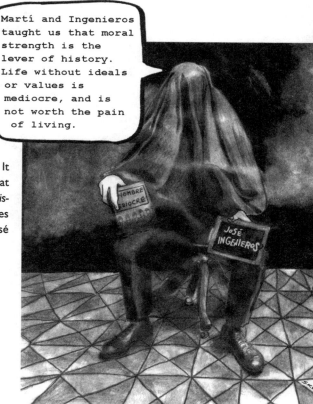

Martí and Ingenieros taught us that moral strength is the lever of history. Life without ideals or values is mediocre, and is not worth the pain of living.

Martí's influence on Fidel's generation

At the root of this anti-imperialist cultural tradition, Martí sets "*Our America*"—Latin America—against the "riotous and brutal North that despises us." He defines the United States, where he lives, as "the monster."

Every day I am in danger of giving my life for my country, and for my duty: through achieving the independence of Cuba, to stop the United States from extending itself into the Antilles and using its strength to dump even more on our American lands. All I do today and all I will ever do is for this. I have lived in the monster and I know its entrails and my sling is David's sling.

Carta a Manuel Mercado, May 18, 1895.

Martí: cultural and social struggle, together!

The struggle for Cuban independence that Martí leads at the end of the nineteenth century combines the task of national liberation with specific plans for transforming society, a radical approach for his time. The republic the Cuban poet dreams of will be inclusive and democratic, by the people and for the people. Blacks and subjugated people will be integrated and emancipated; everyone will stand together in equality. If there is one theoretical and political novelty that links Fidel Castro's leadership style to this field of revolutionary ideas, it is precisely this symbiosis between

Fortunately, our Cuban brother José Martí was able to fight for national American independence in an era when social revolution was already the order of the day.
José de San Martín and Simón Bolívar.

national emancipation and social liberation. This mixture—which takes the struggle for Cuban independence from the snares of imperialism, neocolonialism, and dependence, and weaves it together with the struggle to emancipate the workers—owes its existence to Martí's ideas. In peripheral, semicolonial, and dependent societies, national and social liberation do not happen at different times. The two conditions are reciprocal; they depend on one another. Therefore, the Cuban revolution will be a socialist revolution of national liberation.

Toussaint

Martí reclaimed the legacy of the Haitian Revolution, when we transformed the nation and society at the same time.

Martí and Cuban independence

It is the criminal who promotes a war that can be avoided; and it is the criminal who ignores the war that is inevitable.

José Martí

Cuba has suffered both colonial and neo-colonial domination, first under Spain and later under the United States. Cuba's long process of independence is marked deeply by wars. The first Mambisa War, named for the insurrectionist troops, happens between 1868 and 1878. The second follows in 1879, when an independent battalion refuses to accept either the surrender or the treaty from the first war. The third takes place between 1895 and 1898. After this, the Mambisa War for independence transforms into a war motivated by imperialist robbery when the US intervenes.

Among the principal leaders of Cuban independence: Carlos Manuel de Céspedes (1819–74), who on October 10, 1868, starts an armed battle on his sugar estate, La Demajagua, by crying "Yara!", proclaiming independence, and freeing his slaves; Antonio Maceo (1845–96), a collaborator of Máximo Gómez, who in 1878 rejects, beneath the mangoes of Baraguá and in the face of the Spanish colonialists, the conditions of the peace of Zanjón that ends the first Mambisa War; Máximo Gómez y Báez (1836–1905), a Dominican internationalist who carries out the first machete charge against the Spanish. In 1868, he joins the Cuban movement. In 1892, he joins Martí, and in April 1895, he lands with Martí at Playitas de Cajobabo in Cuba to begin the armed struggle again.

He who intends to seize Cuba will only harvest the ashes of its blood-soaked soil, if he does not perish in the struggle.

Antonio Maceo

Without an awareness of this long tradition, the ideology of Fidel and the Cuban revolution are incomprehensible. As Fidel likes to repeat: "The future of Cuba will be an eternal Baraguá," referring to Maceo's historic protest.

Martí against Spain and the United States

Martí's analysis of the double danger that looms over Cuba—Spanish colonialism and US imperialism—and the way in which he intends to resolve this danger will have huge consequences throughout the twentieth century. The Third World's struggles for liberation are not a question of choosing "the lesser of two evils," of choosing one outside authority over another. Nor does it make sense to fight an external enemy while leaving intact—or even strengthening—an internal enemy. Contemporary social revolutions combine the responsibilities of fighting both transnational monopolies abroad and native capitalists at home.

Cuba: the first modern imperialist war

Martí dies in battle on May 19, 1895. His death, and that of General Antonio Maceo, cripple the Cuban independence process. Shortly afterward, on February 15, 1898, the *USS Maine* explodes in the port of Havana. Two hundred sixty-two crew members die. Various US ships are already on guard close to the Cuban coast as the North American president decides to involve US forces in the war between Cuba and Spain. His objective—as it was in Puerto Rico and the Philippines—is annexation, and to prevent a total victory of the Independents (Mambisa) against the Spanish. The colonial war turns into a conflict between superpowers for an imperialistic share of a colony.

In his famous book, *Imperialism, the Highest Stage of Capitalism*, Lenin (the great leader of the Bolsheviks and the Russian Revolution) classifies the Cuban dispute of 1898, together with the Boer War of 1899–1902, as the "first modern imperialist wars." With the North American intervention in the war, the Revolutionary Cuban Party is dissolved and the Mambisa army disbanded. Spain and the US sign an armistice in Paris. Cuba is excluded from the negotiations.

The Cuban–Spanish–North American war was the first imperialistic war of our time.

The advanced imperialist phase of capitalism

Cuba under the Platt Amendment

In 1901, Leonard Wood, a Yankee military commander, offers an ultimatum: Cuba must accept an amendment to its constitution written by Senator Orville Hitchcock Platt, or Wood's troops will stay on the island permanently. With a vote of sixteen for and eleven against, the Constitutional Assembly approves the Platt Amendment, a legal pretext for intervention and annexation. In addition to appropriating 117.6 square kilometers of Cuban territory (later converted into the military base Guantánamo, which will serve as a Yankee center for torturing prisoners), the US gives itself the right to intervene in Cuban affairs whenever it wants. The bourgeois, neocolonial Cuban Republic is born, "mediated" and controlled by the US. The Yankees govern a native middle class, which combines some economic modernization and capitalist development with racism and dependence. Impotent and subordinate to imperialism (in other words, imperialism's junior partner), this native bourgeoisie has no independent goals or long-term aspirations of its own.

Its politics are bipartisan: conservatives and liberals. Invited by Tomás Estrada Palma, the first president of Cuba (1902–06), the North American troops return to the island in 1906. They remain until 1909, protecting the provisional government established by a North American.

It is the second open intervention by the US. The Cuban presidents that follow—General José Miguel Gómez (1909–20), General Mario García Menocal (1913–20), Alfredo Rayas (1920–24), and Gerardo Machado (1925–33)—remain completely subordinate, making endless concessions and performing whatever troop maneuvers the boss up North orders, in order to avoid a third open intervention.

CUBA AND ITS RICHES BELONG TO US. THIS COLONY IS OUR BACK PATIO. THE BLACKS AND THE MULATTOES ARE INFERIOR AND THEY MUST SERVE US; THE CUBAN WOMEN ARE WHORES.

AMERICA LATINA

United States intervention in Latin America

The Yankee intervention in Cuba—which will last throughout the first half of the twentieth century, until 1959—produces a dependent, controlled, and partially colonized republic. To a greater or lesser degree, this process of imperial domination will repeat itself throughout Latin America to this day.

Yankee interventions in Latin America—including invasions, attacks, assassinations, the planning and funding of coups d'état, and the installation of military bases—are so numerous that it's impossible to list them all in one book. Some of the most important ones include: Nicaragua (1854–55, 1910, 1912, 1933, 1978, 1990), El Salvador (1855, 1980–92), Cuba (1898–1902, 1906–09, 1912, 1917, 1920, 1934, 1952–59, 1959–2006), Puerto Rico (1898–2006), Panama (1903, 1908, 1918, 1925, 1941, 1989), Colombia (1903, 1948, 1966, 2000–06), Dominican Republic (1904, 1916–24, 1963–65), Guatemala (1954, 1980–96), Mexico (1846, 1911, 1914, 1994–2006), Haiti (1915, 1959, 1987–2006), Honduras (1855, 1924, 1979–90), Brazil (1961–64), Paraguay (1954–84, 2004–06), Ecuador (1960–63), Bolivia (1964–75), Chile (1969–90), Uruguay (1969–73), Argentina (1930, 1945–46, 1955, 1962, 1966, 1974–83), Granada (1983), and Venezuela (2002). Imperial domination —and resistance to it—continue all over the South American continent.

We are the masters of the world. Those who oppose us will be considered terrorists and subversives. We will torture them. We will make them disappear.

Mella and the heroic first Cuban Communist Party

On August 16 and 17 of 1925, the first Cuban Communist Party is born, the pre-cursor to the organizations Fidel Castro will found in the 1950s (the July 26th Movement) and 1960s (the second Cuban Communist Party). Julio Antonio Mella (1903–29), the first Party's most brilliant and outstanding figure, participates as a delegate in the Communist Association of Havana, as the party's secretary of propaganda, and as a member of the Central Committee. The founder of the Anti-Clerical League in 1922, the Federation of University Students (FUC) in 1923, and the Anti-Imperialist League in 1925, Mella is one of the fathers of Latin American Marxism, along with the Peruvian José Carlos Maríategui (1894–1930).

For opposing Machado's tyranny, Mella is exiled to Mexico. From there he plans—as Fidel will, years later—an armed expedition to the island to overthrow the dictator-ship. Unlike Fidel's, Mella's plan never takes shape. Machado sends two hired killers to Mexico. They murder Mella with two shots in his back on the night of January 10, 1929. After Mella, the leadership of the first party passes into the hands of Rubén Martínez Villena (1899–1934), the brilliant militant poet. Both Mella's personal hero-ism and the combativeness of that legendary communist party of the 1920s will be among the inspira-tions on which the young Fidel will model himself.

17

Machado's dictatorship and the Revolution of 1933

Gerardo Machado y Morales (1871–1939) comes to power in Cuba in 1925. In 1927, he declares an "Extension of Powers." Although he wants to remain until 1935, his dictatorship falls in 1933.

During the Sixth Pan-American Conference in 1933, the president of the US visits Havana, where a Machadist senator tells him: "The word 'intervention' in my country has been a word of glory, of honor, of triumph, of liberty; it has been independence." Fed up with such displays of bowing and scraping, the Cuban people revolt and force the system into crisis. The insurrection that today we know as the "Revolution of '30" begins. It is embraced by a coalition of rebel groups between 1930 and 1935. In the end, it will be neutralized by North American "mediation."

> Guiteras's "Young Cuba" taught us that there's no dictator who can last 100 years. Armed struggle is the way to socialism and national liberation.

Although the Revolution of 1933 is defeated, it will be the direct model for 1959. Machado flees to the Bahamas; the Yankee envoy to Cuba installs a Machadist minister as president. He does not succeed in stabilizing the country: soldiers, supported by students, spirit him away. A sinister character in Cuba's history appears on the scene: Fulgencio Batista Zaldívar (1901–73). The government becomes the heterogeneous "Pentarchy of 1933"; the Pentarchy also fails to stabilize the country. Finally, Ramón Grau San Martín (1887–1969) is named president, heading a government in which three factions coexist: the Right (Fulgencio Batista), the Center (President Grau), and the Left (Antonio Guiteras). Guiteras, together with Mella, will be two of the major precursors of Fidel Castro's work and actions.

Raúl Roa and the Left Student Wing

Under the dictatorship, the Cuban youth becomes intensely radical. On September 9, 1930, the student Rafael Trejo is killed; in January of 1931, the Left Student Wing (AIE) is born, formed by many members of the Student Revolutionary Directive of '30 (DEU). The AIE gathers together the most radical members, those who follow the policies of Cuban and international communism. Some AIE members are: Aureliano Sánchez Arango, Raúl Roa García, Gabriel Barceló Gomila, Leonardo Fernández Sánchez, and Pablo de la Torriente Brau; all of them are heirs of Mella. A whirlpool of revolutionary thought causes many leftist organizations to break apart and form again; several of these emerge from the newborn communist party. Among the others: the Cuban Revolutionary Anti-Imperialist Organization (ORCA), a clandestine, united, insurrectional group whose secretary general is Pablo de la Torriente Brau, and with whom a young Raúl Roa and Gustavo Alderguía serve; the Lenin Bolshevik Party, a Trotskyite division of the Communist Party, which believes in radical nationalism; and Young Cuba, a nucleus of the anti-imperialist Left, headed by Guiteras.

The popular conscience is ready to try for redemption. Yet this must be preached by bullets. You have the floor, Comrade Mauser!
Raul Roa. October 7, 1931

If Gabriel Barceló is the principal communist student leader of the era after the assassination of Mella, Leonardo Fernández Sánchez is one of the best speakers, Rubén Martínez Villena the grand organizer, Antonio Guiteras the great conspirator, Pablo de la Torriente Brau the most heroic internationalist, and Raúl Roa one of the most brilliant writers of that generation. Like Mella before them and Fidel after them, they try to marry radical anti-imperialism, the non-submissive spirit inherited from Martí, and the fires of revolution Marx's ideas lit in the Caribbean. One of the first Marxist books the young Fidel Castro reads is written by Raúl Roa.

Antonio Guiteras and Young Cuba

During Machado's dictatorship, Guiteras and the other united revolutionaries organize the armed struggle in eastern Cuba. Guiteras leads the insurrection that explodes on April 29, 1933. Guiteras continues the insurrection until the fall of Machado (August 12, 1933), while preparing an attack on the Bayamo military quarter. Later, as minister of President Grau's "government of 100 days" (lasting from September 10, 1933, to January 15, 1934), Guiteras proposes projects such as the nationalization of the North American Electricity Company. During his tenure, the people rebel against the Platt Amendment; Franklin D. Roosevelt (1882–1945) repeals the amendment. Despite this, Cuban sovereignty remains limited, and the territory around the Guantánamo base expands. Meanwhile, Batista plans and leads a coup d'état in January of 1934, imposing presidents whom he selects. The momentum of 1933 fades and the revolution is defeated. After emerging from secrecy and founding Young Cuba, Guiteras is killed in combat at El Morillo, Matanzas, on May 8, 1935, along with Carlos Aponte (an international combatant who had fought with Sandino).

> Our Central Committee supports this idea of imposing a revolutionary government — one ruled by a dictator.

In the 1930s, Guiteras draws forth a radical wellspring of Cuban nationalism. In contrast to other Latin American nationalist movements—escape valves for "channeling" popular revolution; incendiary speeches that defend rule by the bourgeois in ferociously anti-communist terms—Guiteras's movement truly confronts imperialism and the dominant upper classes. On January 20, 1934, Guiteras synthesizes his ideas: "I will fight for the reestablishment of a Government where the rights of Workers and Peasants will be placed above the desires for wealth of National Capitalists and foreigners." His radical thinking and his intransigent anti-imperialism lead him to embrace socialist ideas and armed struggle. Fidel Castro adopts his example.

Antonio Guiteras

The Marxist tradition of Fidel and his predecessors

The Cuban Revolution of 1959 is not a product of four young students, bearded and crazy and in search of adrenaline, as Hollywood movies show. It is a product of all of the rebellions carried out by the Cuban people through their decades of struggle against North American imperialism and the military dictatorships of the native capitalists. Although commercial biographies of Fidel Castro and Hollywood scriptwriters both disavow it, this long accumulation of experiences and radical thought—the heritage of Martí, along with the Marxist revolutionaries of the 1920s and 1930s, including Mella, Martínez Villena, Roa, Guiteras, and others—have been fundamental to Fidel's education. He derives his Marxist ideas from these, long before his 1960s alliance with the Soviet Union.

In addition to the *Communist Manifesto* by Marx and Engels (which Fidel reads during the third year of his law career), *The History of Worker Legislation*, and several essays about the historiography of political ideas, the young Fidel's first radical speeches are influenced by the work of the young Raúl Roa (who in addition to being a member of the AIE will years later become a chancellor of the Cuban revolution and Fidel's friend).

One of the Marxist books Fidel reads as a student is Roa's first volume of *History of Social Doctrines* (1949). In these years, from 1949 onward, the young Fidel will acquire the entire series of Marxist titles on Carlos III Street, where the Socialist Party of the People (PSP) library can be found. He borrows the books and keeps them; at the time, he has no way to pay for them.

In the university I learned the best things in my life: I became a follower of Martí and a revolutionary. In the Law School I was nurtured on the revolutionaries of the 1930s; I adopted the ideas of Marx and Lenin.

University Reform in Fidel's time

Accompanied by the example of his predecessors of the 1920s and '30s, the young student Fidel Castro becomes a revolutionary at the university. There he soaks up a universe of anti-imperialist culture from the University Reform movement. While Fidel frequents the hill of the University of Havana, the idea of completely rejecting all Yankee interference gains ground among the students, and in the departments of the contentious professors they admire.

We are ready for the revolution. We are living in a Latin American age. The future belongs to the young anti-imperialists, not to the mediocrities.

We need to organize the Latin American Union against imperialism. The young have a fundamental role. We must learn from the Bolsheviks.

University Reform is born in Córdoba, Argentina, in 1918, inspired by Deodora Roca (1890–1942) and his mentor, José Ingenieros. It later spreads throughout the continent, and in Cuba a version is adopted that privileges Latin Americanism and the rebellious role the youth play in the struggle against North American rule.

Martínez Villena

Ideals versus the "Mediocre Man"

In confronting the mediocre man of capitalism, we need to reassert the new ideals of the Russian Revolution, new values, and a new ethic.

José Ingenieros

There is a direct link between the ideology of Argentinean University Reform and the Cuban precursors on whom Fidel models himself. In 1925, Ingenieros, returning from Mexico, meets in Havana with Mella, Martínez Villena, and Gustavo Aldereguía. Much later, after the death of the mentor of his youth, Martínez Villena writes an article titled "On the Occasion of the Death of José Ingenieros" as part of a debate with Jorge Mañach. Even Raúl Roa and Mariátegui describe Ingenieros as one of their principal mentors.

In contrast to the "official" interpretations of socialism by the USSR and similar countries—where economics and the role of class struggle are the predominant ideology—the Cuban revolution promotes, from the beginning, an ethical and cultural concept of socialism. Both Fidel's emphasis on revolutionary ethics and on living out ideals and Che Guevara's concepts of the "new man" and moral incentives grew in a common womb. The influence of *The Mediocre Man* and *Moral Strength*, both books by Ingenieros, as well as the other ideological nuclei linked to University Reform, are indispensable to understanding this new Latin American reading of Marxism.

Master: All the future needs to be better.

Julio Mella

Ethics in young Fidel's political thinking

The ethical ideals that brand the young Fidel remain unchanged throughout his entire political career. Half a century after his early training, in the beginning of the twenty-first century, Fidel continues to insist in many speeches that the suffering of the people under capitalism should not be measured only in material terms—by the low number of calories ingested daily in impoverished areas—but also in moral terms: humiliation, scorn, low self-esteem, indifference, marginalization. The same applies when, as in his speech of November 17, 2005, Fidel questions the corruption, the increasing wealth of the wealthy, the class differences, the loss of moral fiber, and the egoism that the market generates when it tries to coexist with socialism.

Faced with the filthy power of money, gold, and the cruelty of the market, we reassert dignity, rebellion, patriotism, the self-esteem of the people, and moral revolution. An honest man doesn't follow the ethical code under which he'll live better, but rather the code which is his duty.

Fidel at the university

Although the cultural atmosphere of University Reform promotes anti-imperialism, the university where Fidel studies is controlled completely by an officious, gangster-like mafia in the service of the government of the moment. This group carries guns and exerts control over the university grounds. At this time Fidel enjoys a reputation for his youth and his studiousness. The mafia stops him from entering the university grounds. He confronts them—at first without weapons, later with them—from a political position that is progressive, anti-imperialist, and radical, but still, at this point, his position and his alone. He doesn't yet have a group to support him.

If Ulysses was enchanted by the songs of sirens, the university hill was seduced by communist ethics and the truths of Marxism. I am prepared to earn the hate of some thousands, among them some of my relatives, half of my acquaintances, two-thirds of my professional colleagues, and four-fifths of my college friends.

Recognizing the anti-imperialist tradition of University Reform, during 1947 Fidel presides over the Pro-Dominican Democracy Committee and the Pro-Liberation of Puerto Rico Committee, maintaining a relationship with the leader of the independence movement, Pedro Albizu Campos (1893–1965). As part of this anti-imperialist impulse, Fidel enlists as a soldier in a campaign—ultimately a frustrated campaign—to overthrow the Dominican dictator Trujillo. His contingent trains in Cayo Confites in the north of Cuba. There, Fidel is first named the lieutenant of his squad, and later the commander of one of the companies in the battalion. Already, in 1947, he has a plan in mind to begin a guerrilla war in the mountains of Santo Domingo.

Fidel and the Bogotá Rebellion

Just as the young Che Guevara (1928–67) experienced at first hand, before Cuba, both the Bolivian Revolution of 1952 and the Guatemala Process of 1954 (aborted due to Yankee intervention), Fidel Castro also lives through two Latin American rebellions before the Cuban Revolution. The first is the revolutionary expedition to the Dominican Republic, in which Fidel enlists as an international soldier in 1947. The second is the Bogotá Rebellion in 1948, in which he is an active participant. He is twenty-two years old.

Traveling in Venezuela, Panama, and Colombia, Fidel tries to organize a Latin American congress of fellow students to oppose the meetings of the Organization of American States (OAS), which is under the control of the United States. In Colombia he meets Jorge Eliecer Gaitán (1903– 48), the popular leader who opposes the Colombian political tradition of *caciques*, bosses. Gaitán is murdered in Bogotá on April 9, 1948, minutes before returning to meet for a second time with Fidel Castro. The masses' spontaneous revolt, provoked by the murder, becomes the Bogotá Rebellion; it culminates in an "agreement" between the bourgeois leaders and the betrayal of the people's expectations. In the middle of the fighting in the streets, Fidel helps to form a squadron of insurrectionist fighters. He even becomes an assistant to the chief of police, who rises up against the army.

In Colombia, in 1948, I understood:
#1. The murderous ferocity of the Latin American solidiers in the service of the powerful and of imperialism.
#2. The heroism of the people isn't enough without political education, strategy, and organization.

Two decades of humiliation

The Cuban revolution of 1933 fails, and the impulse among the people that originally gave rise to it is diverted. The following two decades are marked by corruption, gangsterism, and the dependence of the bourgeois republic on the United States. Pushed and pulled in different directions, the Cuban bourgeoisie, un-

able to free the country, try to maintain their rule for almost twenty years. Under the neocolonial system, several governments follow: Carlos Manuel de Céspedes y Quesada (1933); Ramón Grau San Martín (1933–34); Carlos Mendieta (1934–35); Miguel Mariano Gómez (1936); Federico Laredo Bru (1936–40); Fulgencio Batista (1940–44); Ramón Grau San Martín (1944–48); Carlos Prío Socarrás (1948–52), and again, following a coup d'état, Batista (1952–59). As it is throughout colonial societies, imperialism's troops humiliate and degrade the subjugated people. The same continues throughout these decades, reaching a climax on March 11, 1949, when several US soldiers desecrate a statue of José Martí. These are years of fierce anti-communism, during which the Cuban bourgeoisie jail and repress selfless working-class leaders, such as the Communist Union leaders Jesús Menéndez (murdered January 22, 1948) and Aracelio Iglesias Díaz (murdered October 17, 1948). The anti-imperialist rejection of North American domination deepens among the people. This same year, during a protest against the United States marines, a student is savagely beaten. The young Fidel Castro, at this time the head of the Federation of University Students (FEU), is a witness to the beating and denounces the act. The arrogance and humiliations multiply every weekend, when the marines use Cuba as their place for "fun."

The Orthodox Party and Chibás

Eduardo René Chibás Rivas (1907–51) had, in the 1920s, been the leader of the Student Revolutionary Directory, fighting against the dictator Machado and the "Extension of Powers." Much later, he is a member of the Authentic Cuban Revolutionary Party. In 1947, discontented and frustrated with Grau's government, Chibás creates a new political organization: the Orthodox Party of the Cuban People. The new party has eighty thousand members in Havana alone. Chibás is elected senator in 1950. He denounces the corruption of the government, using the radio as his propaganda instrument. One of his most famous slogans is *"Shame On Money!"*

Having accused Aureliano Sánchez Arango, the minister of education under President Prío, of owning properties in Guatemala, and having been unable to prove the accusation, Chibás feels cornered. He grows depressed, and on August 5, 1951, he commits suicide. He shoots himself in the stomach during his final Sunday night radio show; he finishes his final speech by saying: "People of Cuba, wake up! This is my last warning!" (On July 2, 1953, Fidel carries a tape of this speech with him when he attacks the Moncada barracks.) After Chibás's death, the Orthodox Party, leaning toward populism, continues trying to gain power through elections. Their platform is based on economic independence, political liberty, and social justice. From 1951 on, the young Fidel's actions move to the left of the Orthodox Party.

Young Fidel and political struggle

Before launching himself into an armed struggle, the young Fidel tries to develop a mass political movement through legal means. He puts himself forward as a candidate for the House of Representatives. He publishes his denunciation of government corruption in the newspaper *Alerta* and covers 40,000 to 50,000 kilometers in a Chevy 50-315—bought on credit—for his political campaign.

Fidel has studied military history and the history of war since he was a boy. He immerses himself in the battles of the French Revolution and the Cuban Wars of Independence, but always keeping in mind that politics rules over war, and that all war—even revolutionary war—is political.

29

Batista's coup d'état

The coup d'état of March 10, 1952—which overthrows Carlos Prío Socarrás (1948–52) and imposes the dictatorship of Fulgencio Batista—is the soil in which the 1959 Cuban Revolution will grow.

The emergence of the new Batista dictatorship in Cuba will provide evidence of the crisis of legitimacy that plagues the neocolonial republic, and of the incapacity of the Cuban bourgeoisie's political system to maintain minimal civil liberties. The Latin American capitalists represent the true face of the system, which, under a banner of "free world," "open society," "democracy," and "pluralism," has, throughout the twentieth century and across the South American continent, imposed repression, persecution, censorship, torture, and systematic violations of human rights.

WE DEFEND THE NATIONAL SECURITY OF THE UNITED STATES AND ITS LOCAL PARTNERS: THE NATIVE BOURGOISIE.

Dream Team: Batista, Duvalier, Stroessner, Pinochet, Somoza, CIA agents, Videla, Trujillo, Banzer.

Batista: a populist dictator

Of humble origins, Batista is born in Banes. He enlists in the army in 1921, and by 1933 he has already led a coup d'état. With Grau San Martín, he becomes the commander of the army, thus maintaining control of the country during various governments. Elected president in 1940, he broadens his populist framework of alliances, even dragging along the PSP, and achieves some social reforms, including the somewhat modern 1940 constitution. In 1944, the candidate that Batista nominates is defeated. Batista remains in the background, living in Florida until 1948. In 1952, he leads a new coup d'état against Prío Socarrás. His dictatorship, cruel and soaked in blood—and supported by the US—lasts seven years, until the triumph of the 1959 revolution. On January 1, 1959, he flees to the Dominican Republic under the dictator Trujillo and later dies in Franco's Spain.

After the death of Mella and Martínez Villena, the direction of the class-conscious, heroic, and radically anti-imperialist Cuban Communist Party was abandoned. Following the International Communists and the Soviet Communist Party under Joseph Stalin (1879–1953), in 1935 the Cuban Communist Party first left behind its "popular front" politics and later went directly to "national unity." They rebaptized themselves as the Socialist Party of the People (PSP). In 1940, the PSP ended by making an alliance, "in the name of this national unity"—with Batista! Trying to find a mature balance for Cuban communism, Fidel asserts: "In Cuba it seemed appropriate that a Marxist-Leninist party [the PSP] was allied to a bloody, repressive, and corrupt government like Batista's ... this contradiction logically caused many of the young, people with revolutionary inclinations as well as people on the left, to stop sympathizing with the Cuban Marxist-Leninist party. That is the objective historical reality." (Speech of September 4, 1995)

LATIN AMERICAN DICTATORS ARE SONS OF BITCHES, BUT THEY'RE OUR SONS OF BITCHES.

Prostitution, gambling, and the Mafia

In Batista's day, Cuba turns into a gigantic casino. The mafia has no limits; this is their glorious golden age. Whorehouses and cultural degradation spread. In contrast to the films of Francis Ford Coppola (like the *Godfather* trilogy), the Cuban Mafia is far from being poetic or from having any code of honor whatsoever. This is the "Golden Cuba" that the far-right extremists in Miami yearn for even today.

Miami, a "prosperous" colony

To counteract the influence of the Cuban revolution of 1959, US government publications tout Miami, land of Latin American immigrants, as an example for the whole continent to imitate. Using Hollywood and the monopoly machinery of global (mis)communication, they present Florida as a prosperous, utopian immigrant community even today. A submissive and obedient servant, having forgotten his own identity and his own culture, can rise in terms of money and business by accepting the imperial master, by imitating his "American way of life."

Miami and the Mafia

The Mafia, with its network of families, was born in the rural parts of southern Italy. Some of its members immigrate to the US in the nineteenth century, and during the 1920s they begin to build their network of North American power. If during Prohibition in the 1920s they focus on alcohol, much later they extend their power into gambling, prostitution, and drugs. An important section of the North American Mafia has its base of operations in neocolonial Cuba. In the 1950s, they build massive luxury hotels in Havana. Faced with the victory of the 1959 Cuban Revolution, the Mafia, the cream of Havana's bourgeoisie, will immigrate to Miami. There they will merge and mingle with the extreme right portion of the Cuban immigrant population.

We, the Mafia, need capitalism like the fish need water to live in.

The mafiosos are "freedom fighters" and we should support them with money and weapons against the Communists and other trouble-makers.

The Cuban Mafia in Miami will not only participate in the assassination of John F. Kennedy (November 22, 1963), they will also try many times to assassinate Fidel Castro. As part of their extreme right politics, they will support state terrorism in Latin America with money and spies, perpetuating several military dictatorships through the sinister Operation Condor. In addition, they will be involved—according to Fidel himself, in his 2008 autobiography *Mi vida*—in manipulating the 2000 presidential elections in the United States to install George W. Bush in the presidency, illegally and against the will of the majority of the United States' people.

The protests of the young

To confront Batista's 1952 coup, which increases the power of the Mafia, students return to the streets. One of the first protests deposits the "corpse" of the constitution, trodden on by the military, in front of the statue of Martí. In another, on January 28, 1953, the crowds shout "Revolution!" on the centennial anniversary of Martí's birth. Fidel secretly edits the newspaper *El Acusador*. Referring to the Orthodox Party, he writes: "A revolutionary party deserves a revolutionary leadership, young and from the people, which will save Cuba." With the help of the FEU, Fidel begins secretly training fifteen hundred students, or one hundred fifty combat units, in the revolutionary system developed by Chibás. The best of these will participate later in the attack on the Moncada barracks.

The young people's attack on Moncada in 1953 marks a turning point in twentieth-century thinking and politics in Latin America. With this gesture—which is not meant to chase some easy and meaningless victory, but rather to mobilize public opinion, to delegitimize agreements with the dictatorship, to strike a blow against the enemy, to obtain weapons, and to initiate the revolutionary process—the young people point to armed struggle as a strategic option. They do not launch the insurgency as some irrational search for an adrenalin rush. On the contrary, they begin with a political confrontation that stretches into a political and military battle. Between Batista's coup of March 10, 1952, and the July 26, 1953, attack at Moncada, a year and four months of intense political training takes place.

Fidel's leadership and the young people at Moncada

Before leaving for Santiago de Cuba, the young people come to meetings in the apartment shared by Haydée Santamaría Cuadrado (1922–80) and her brother, Abel Santamaría Cuadrado (1927–53), both comrades of Fidel. There they make plans and preparations. Less than ten know beforehand that their objective is Moncada. Most of the young people who attack Moncada come from the left wing of the Orthodox Party, which is in the middle of a dizzying political radicalization. In addition to the Santamaría siblings, there are José Luis Tasende de las Muñecas, Pedro Miret, Renato Guitart Rosell, and Raúl Gómez García (all of whom will die in the attack), Jesús Montané, Ramiro Valdés, José Suárez, Raúl Castro, Oscar Alcalde, Pedro Marrero, Gustavo Arcos, José Ponce, Abelardo Crespo, Fideo Labrador, and Fernando Chenard, among many others.

In his later years, Fidel Castro will remember that if, at the time of the Bogotá Uprising in 1948, he has an anti-imperialist conscience, by the time of the Moncada attack in 1953 he possesses strong Marxist-Leninist convictions. Recognizing this mature balance, he will recall: "One could say that it takes six years to acquire a revolutionary conscience and to develop a revolutionary strategy."

The attack on the Moncada barracks

One hundred and twenty-two young students, the best of the fifteen hundred trained by Fidel, arrive in secret at Santiago de Cuba. Among the fighters are two women: Haydée Santamaría Cuadrado (1922–80) and Melba Hernández Rodríguez del Rey (b. 1921). The attack begins at 5:15 a.m. on July 26, 1953. They intend to take the most important fortress in Santiago de Cuba, the second-most important in the country, in order to unite the people and call a general

Aerial view of the Moncada barracks.

Youths who participated in the attack. In the center of the photo, Raúl Castro.

strike against the dictatorship. They divide the task. Abel Santamaría leads twenty-one fighters who try to take the public hospital and Raúl Castro (b.1931), with ten others, tries to attack the courthouse. Both groups find themselves stuck at the Moncada barracks, which Fidel attacks with ninety-five men. The attack fails; there is no element of surprise. There are fifty-three dead, according to some reports, more than eighty, according to others, including the dead from Moncada and those from the Bayamo barracks.

After a quarter century of unchallenged Stalinism on the continent—during which the concept of a revolution by stages, the separation between anti-imperialism and socialism, and the illusion of a "peaceful transition to socialism" all dominate—the attack on Moncada triggers an unprecedented popular uprising across Latin America. The political map shifts; the idea that power belongs exclusively to the enemies of the people changes. Because of the Moncada attack, the heroic traditions of the early Latin American Marxism of the 1920s are taken up again. Moncada will contribute to the flowering of revolutions in Latin America during the 1960s.

Torture and murder

In the fallout of the failed attack on Moncada, many young people are caught, tortured, and killed. Moncada becomes a factory for torture and murder. The disproportionate number of deaths among the defenders and the attackers stands as evidence of a brutal massacre: a usual practice of Latin American dictatorships, in which the lives and rights of captured prisoners are never respected. The two female fighters survive, although their arms are burned with cigarettes.

Abel Santamaría Cuadrado (1927–53) accompanies Fidel on his political campaigns. Jesús Montané Oropesa (1923–99), another Moncada fighter, had introduced them on August 16, 1952. In the attack, Abel, Fidel's second-in-command, is taken prisoner. Minutes before, Abel says to his companions: "Save the two women; all of us will be killed. Understand that each small gesture we make will become a historic act. I would prefer to keep living, but destiny asks me to die for Cuba. Know that we are worthy of our mission; die knowing that we have been useful to history."

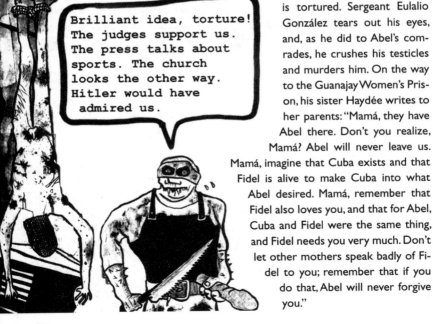

Brilliant idea, torture! The judges support us. The press talks about sports. The church looks the other way. Hitler would have admired us.

Defenseless and unarmed, he is tortured. Sergeant Eulalio González tears out his eyes, and, as he did to Abel's comrades, he crushes his testicles and murders him. On the way to the Guanajay Women's Prison, his sister Haydée writes to her parents: "Mamá, they have Abel there. Don't you realize, Mamá? Abel will never leave us. Mamá, imagine that Cuba exists and that Fidel is alive to make Cuba into what Abel desired. Mamá, remember that Fidel also loves you, and that for Abel, Cuba and Fidel were the same thing, and Fidel needs you very much. Don't let other mothers speak badly of Fidel to you; remember that if you do that, Abel will never forgive you."

Che Guevara on Moncada

On July 26, 1967, many years after the victory of the Cuban revolution, while fighting in Bolivia for the freedom of all America, Che Guevara writes a concise but profound analysis in his journal of what the attack on the Moncada barracks means to the people across Latin America.

The attack on Moncada is not only a political act. As Che Guevara points out in his *Bolivian Diary*, at the same time it has theoretical consequences. In truth, it provokes an argument about the passivity of the many strains of the traditional Left, which, in the name of a "lack of meaningful conditions" for revolution, ends by entirely adapting itself to the established order, accepting it as something fated and unchangeable.

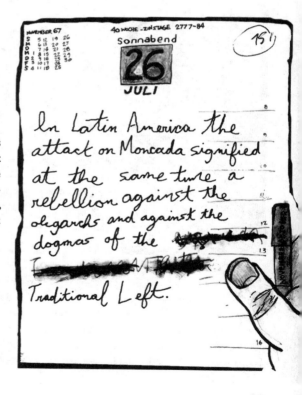

NOVEMBER 67
S   5 12 19 26
M   6 13 20 27
T   7 14 21 28
W 1 8 15 22 29
T 2 9 16 23 30
F 3 10 17 24
S 4 11 18 25

40 WOCHE - ZINSTAGE 2777~84

Sonnabend

26

JULI

In Latin America the attack on Moncada signified at the same time a rebellion against the oligarchs and against the dogmas of the ~~Traditional Left~~ Traditional Left.

The Cold War during the attack on Moncada

At the time of the Moncada attack, the world is in the middle of the Cold War. As World War II ends with the victory of the Allies over Nazi Germany, the US and the USSR confront each other, establishing their respective "spheres of influence." In 1949, the Chinese Revolution triumphs, and in 1950, the Korean War breaks out, which, due to Yankee intervention, divides the country in two. The US sees its world power threatened, which makes it "harden" internally. Senator Joseph Raymond McCarthy (1908–57) rides the crest of a wave of personal accusations, cultural persecution, and the violation of democratic liberties.

On March 5, 1953, Stalin dies. This begins a period of "thaw" and of collaboration with North American imperialism. Prior to that, Stalin moderates Soviet foreign policy. For example, abandoning the tradition of Lenin, he dissolves the International Communist Party in 1943. In the 1950s, the Soviets neither support nor repudiate Latin American rebellions—much less armed struggles for radical change. Those under Soviet influence in Latin America do not view the Moncada assault with sympathy.

The traditional Left responds to Moncada

In the 1950s, around the time of Moncada, the organizations of the traditional Left follow the Soviet doctrine of "Peaceful Transition to Socialism" (which coincides with the division of areas of influence between the US and the USSR). From this point forward, these pro-Soviet groups maintain that conditions are not ripe either for an armed struggle or for socialism in Latin America. The Moncada attack and the Cuban revolution taken together shatter these "revolutionary dogmas," according to Che Guevara's characterization.

In Cuba, the pro-Soviet PSP condemns Moncada. In his August 30, 1953 "Letter to The Militants," the executive committee of the PSP denounces the attack as a "rabble-rousing, undisciplined, desperate initiative, typical of a petty bourgeoisie without principles and compromised by gangsterism." In their "Weekly Letter" of October 20, 1953, they insist that the Moncada assault was "a putsch" and "a desperate, armed act, in the category of an adventure." These actions "lead to nothing but disaster, wasted effort, and meaningless death." In June of 1957, six months after the *Granma* landing, issue 149 of the PSP's magazine *Foundations* will persist in condemning Fidel: "It is important to continue to affirm…that today as yesterday, we repudiate and condemn and continue to condemn terrorist and putsch-like methods as inefficient, noxious, and contrary to the interests of the people." Without forgetting these facts, a mature Fidel—putting unity first—would generously point out: "In spite of this… in my youth I read books from the PSP's library."

We must respect order and peaceful coexistence.

Castro and his friends are adventurers. There are inevitable laws in a society. Cuba isn't prepared for a revolution.

BE REALISTS: ONLY ASK FOR WHAT'S POSSIBLE

Judgment

The first oral judicial hearing is September 21, 1953. Filed under the name "Lawsuit 37," the young attackers explain the assault and denounce the murder and torture of their comrades. In his plea, later known as *History Will Absolve Me*, Fidel Castro maintains: "Only José Martí should be linked with the action, since he is its intellectual author" (Plea of October 16, 1953). When the public prosecutor shows a book by Lenin with which to accuse him, Fidel responds: "Yes, we read Lenin, and whoever doesn't read Lenin is an ignoramus" (Fidel's recollection, from speech of April 22, 1970). Fidel Castro and twenty-eight other combatants, among them Juan Almeida and Fidel's brother Raúl, receive sentences of up to fifteen years in prison.

In his cell after the trial, Fidel reconstructs his oral plea piece by piece. Isolated and under heavy guard, he rewrites, page by page, the text of his defense. He uses thin pages of onion-skin paper that relatives of his fellow prisoners sneak out of the prison secretly, in the bottom of small matchboxes. He writes in almost microscopic letters and with the juice of a lemon; his writing only turns visible when the paper is heated. In these difficult conditions, taking José Martí as inspiration, *History Will Absolve Me* is born, the programmatic and propagandistic text of the future July 26th Movement.

History Will Absolve Me

In *History Will Absolve Me*, Fidel changes from the accused to the accuser. His reasoning and his prose are written in the ancient tradition of critical thinking: thinking as a weapon to denounce power and the status quo. Fidel's gesture takes on the manner of Emile Zola's celebrated *J'accuse*, the modern archetype of intellectuals confronting the established power. But in contrast to Zola, who fought against the military and government of his time, Fidel's work is not merely a denunciation. As he criticizes the regime's crimes and legitimizes rebellion, he also explains the logic behind the Moncada attack (condensed into five laws for future revolutionaries). Grounding himself in a sociological analysis of Cuban society, Fidel proposes radical changes without yet mentioning socialism.

You've made Cuba into a North American colony. Condemn me, it doesn't matter! HISTORY WILL ABSOLVE ME!

In this book, Fidel puts forward his sociological analysis of the people. To analyze them, he breaks them down into their different social classes. His presentation is not cold, like a census, but rather a dynamic conception of a "struggling people," repeating several times: "It is the struggle we speak of." In his view, the Cuban people in 1953 consist of: a) 400,000 industrial workers and laborers, b) 500,000 agricultural workers, c) 600,000 unemployed, d) 100,000 small farmers, e) 30,000 teachers and professors, f) 20,000 small commercial businessmen overwhelmed by debt, and g) 10,000 young professionals. Fidel does not include the native bourgeoisie among the people: this is fundamental! This shows the difference between Fidel's ideas and the platforms of both the traditional left and populist nationalism, as both of these ended by making alliances with this same bourgeoisie.

Fidel in prison

After sentencing, Fidel and his comrades are locked away in a hospital wing of the prison on Isla de Pinos.

Two years later, Batista's dictatorship needs to earn popular support. Under pressure from the people, who shout for Fidel and his comrades' freedom, Batista decrees an amnesty for the prisoners. They are released on May 15, 1955.

Release from prison

They have money and power. The US supports them. But we will win. Our ethics are unswerving and our will indomitable. That makes us invincible.

Immediately after his release, Fidel reorganizes his forces and founds the July 26th Movement. In 1955, before his exile, he declares: "In 1956 we will be free or we will be martyrs." All the eyes of the dictatorship settle on the amnestied insurgents. To reorganize themselves, they must leave Cuba. They decide on Mexico. There, outside of the island, they organize a political and military movement to continue their struggle. Their first manifesto is published on August 8, 1955.

Although Fidel and his comrades are based in Mexico, one of the first countries the young Cuban politician visits is the United States. He goes in October of 1955. There, he affirms: "In Cuba, the exact same thing is happening as happened in 1868 and 1895. You would have to be blind not to see it." (Speech of October 10, 1955)

Believe in Fidel: Behind bars, we continue to be revolutionaries.

Antonio Gramsci

The July 26th Movement and the problem of the party

Some European intellectuals will point out: "The Cuban revolution happened without having a political party." Curiously, they will forget the July 26th Movement. Its militancy is nurtured by the young leftists of the Orthodox Party, led by Eduardo Chibás, and the National Revolutionary Movement (MNR), led by Rafael García Bárcena (1907–61). Chibás kills himself; Bárcena is arrested and tortured. When Fidel forms the July 26th Movement, he declares it to be "the revolutionary apparatus of Chibásism" (Fidel's letter to the Congress of Orthodox Militants, August 16, 1955), but later he breaks from the Orthodox Party in March of 1956. Thus the July 26th Movement acquires intellectual autonomy and becomes a vanguard revolutionary organization. Even when some groups stir up anti-communist sentiment, the Movement's principal leaders, Fidel Castro and Ernesto Che Guevara, follow the ideas of Marx and Lenin.

In 1966, Fidel will explain the problem of party in the Cuban Revolution: "We do not deny the importance of the Party, the Organization, the Movement, or whatever it's called. But it's not a party just because it calls itself 'Party.' A party is not Marxist-Leninist because it once signed the name 'Marxist-Leninist' on the property register. To create a revolution requires a Marxist-Leninist party or organization, a revolutionary organization. Gentlemen, if there is a Marxist-Leninist Party that knows every passage in *Das Kapital* and everything Marx, Engels, and Lenin have written by heart—and that Party 'doesn't do a lick of work,' as they say in the people's language and Creole ... other people aren't allowed to create the revolution? Those who want to create the revolution—aren't they an organization, a party?" (Speech of August 29, 1966)

He wants to have a revolution without a Party.

Fidel is a heretic.

46

In exile in Mexico

In Mexico, Fidel and his comrades begin to form military units, preparing for a clandestine insurrection. There they gather money and weapons, they train themselves, and they prepare themselves for the return to the island. At one point they are reported to the immigration authorities and the entire group is detained. Their weapons are seized. Later they are quickly released. (The one whose release is delayed the most is Guevara, who—in front of the police—declares himself a communist!)

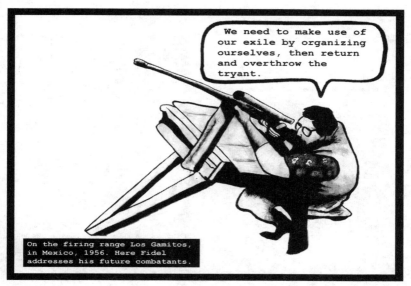

On the firing range Los Gamitos, in Mexico, 1956. Here Fidel addresses his future combatants.

In Cuban history, there have been a number of insurrectionist groups who planned an armed invasion of the island in order to overthrow different tyrants. The oldest example is José Martí, who in April of 1895 succeeds in his plan of landing at Playitas de Cajobabo in order to resume the armed struggle against the Spanish. He is not successful, and dies in the fight. Later, in the 1920s, Julio Antonio Mella (also exiled in Mexico) plans an identical invasion, hoping to overthrow Machado's dictatorship. He doesn't succeed; he is assassinated. Finally, Fidel and the July 26th Movement again take up the task with the same plan: invade Cuba by sea and overthrow Batista's military dictatorship. This third invasion is the one that will finally succeed.

The Latin American view

In June of 1954, in Guatemala, the United States achieves a well-known ambition. They conspire against a democratic government and prepare a mercenary invasion—under the command of Colonel Carlos Castillo Armas—to defend the interests of the big corporations, including the infamous United Fruit, specializing in bananas. The invasion overthrows the legitimate government of Jacobo Árbenz. Árbenz's inability to defend himself against the power of the CIA and its mercenaries makes an impression on an entire generation of young Latin American anti-imperialists. Among these is Fidel Castro.

Guatemala is ours, like the rest of Latin America.

The coup d'état in Guatemala and the Yankee invasion demonstrate that in Latin America, armed struggle is the only viable way.

Guatemala is not an isolated event; the influence of this and other Latin American incidents will be inestimable. In *History Will Absolve Me*, Fidel notes: "The case of Bolivia is very recent, where the miners, with rolls of dynamite, crushed and destroyed the regiments of the regular army."

First meeting with Ernesto Guevara

Fidel Castro and Ernesto Guevara meet for the first time in Mexico through Nico López, a Cuban militant whom Guevara knew in Guatemala. The meeting takes place in the home of María Antonia González, a Cuban woman married to a Mexican, in whose apartment the exiled Cubans conspire. Guevara meets Raúl Castro first, who at this time has already openly declared himself a Marxist, and later he meets Raúl's brother Fidel. Fidel and Ernesto dine alone for hours, and at the end of the meeting, Fidel gains a doctor for the July 26th Movement.

In one of his letters, the young Ernesto writes: "Meeting Fidel Castro is a political accomplishment: a Cuban revolutionary, a young man, very intelligent, very sure of himself, extraordinarily audacious; I believe we have a mutual sympathy." The Cubans quickly baptize Guevara as "Che," making reference to his Argentinean accent. The same night that Che joins the July 26th Movement, he makes Fidel promise that once the Cuban revolution succeeds, Fidel will allow him to leave Cuba and return to fight in Argentina. Fidel agrees.

Fidel and Che: an unconquerable friendship

The Cuban Revolution has the good fortune of counting on not just one, but two great historical figures. Although the two companions will share many revolutionary experiences—from fighting together in the Sierra Maestra to studying Marx's *Das Kapital* together in the early years of the revolutionary government—each has a side that complements the other.

- Hey, Fidel. What do you think of studying Marx's *Das Kapital* and Lenin's *The State and the Revolution* together?
- Yeah, man, I completely agree. Let's also read Martí, Bolivar, Antonio Guiteras, and Mella.

If Fidel is the principal leader and political strategist of the revolution, as well as an incomparably charismatic orator, Che—in addition to being the "heroic guerrilla and fighter"—is without a doubt the major writer of Marxist theory. In both, the anti-imperialist thought of Latin America and revolutionary Marxism are joined and mixed together—two traditions that have never before been united in other social movements on the continent.

Cuba's internationalist tradition

That the Argentinean Ernesto Che Guevara, a "foreigner," will come to be, along with Fidel, the great leader of the Cuban revolution, is not a rare occurrence in Cuban history. There are many precedents. In Martí's day and during the war with Spain, one of the Cuban leaders is Máximo Gómez y Báez, a Dominican internationalist. Much later, in Mexico, when the July 26th Movement prepares itself for the *Granma* expedition, one of its main instructors is "Angelito" (Albert Bayo), an ex-colonel of the Spanish Republic exiled in Mexico, teacher to Fidel, Raúl, and Che Guevara on questions of strategy and war.

This internationalist tradition isn't restricted to either Martí's or Fidel's generation. Between the two can be found the generation of the the 1920s and '30s. One of that generation's major figures is Pablo de la Torriente Brau, who dies in Spain fighting in the celebrated Fifth Regiment against Franco's followers. Death finds him, between Majadahonda and Romanillos, on the cold morning of December 18, 1936. A fascist bullet tears his chest and leaves through his back. He gives his life for the Spanish Republic and for world revolution, in the ranks of a battalion led by another Cuban internationalist, Policarpo Candón. De la Torriente Brau is buried in Barcelona. Many years later, continuing this long tradition, Cuba will send thousands and thousands of internationalists to fight in Asia, Africa, and Latin America.

The *Granma* expedition

Fidel leads an insurgent expedition that sails on November 25, 1956, from the port of Tuxpan in Mexico: its destination Cuba, its objective to continue the battle begun with the attack on the Moncada barracks and to overthrow the military dictatorship. The expedition travels for seven days on the *Granma*, a small yacht not designed to transport eighty-two people by sea. The men and women of the expedition suffer from nausea, vomiting, and a thousand complaints. When they arrive at the island, Che Guevara and Raúl Castro are the last to disembark.

On November 30, 1956, led by Frank País, the young men of the July 26th Movement from the cities—known as "el llano" to distinguish them from the people from the rural areas, known as "la sierra"—throw themselves into taking the city of Santiago de Cuba. The attack by "el llano" is to be synchronized with the *Granma*'s arrival, but the boat comes nearly three days late, on December 2, and by then the Cuban army has already been alerted and deployed in the area where the eighty-two fighters on the *Granma* land at the Coloradas Beach at the Pico Turquino cove in the far southwest of Cuba. Those who arrive successfully escape into the mountainous region of the Sierra Maestra.

Fidel, master of enthusiasm

Upon arriving, Fidel's followers split up. Batista's army is ready for them. They pursue Fidel's group through the fields of cane plantations. The first battle is known as "Alegría de Pío," Pío's Happiness. Three from the expedition die, two in combat and one later from a mortal wound. Another is seriously wounded. During the pursuit, the army murders eighteen prisoners of war. The people protest the crime; the lives of the remaining twenty-one revolutionaries are spared, and they are sent to prison instead. Twenty succeed in escaping to the city. Of these, seven will later rejoin Fidel in the mountains. The rest, led by Fidel, arrive in the Sierra Maestra. In all, of the eighty-two from the *Granma* expedition, only seventeen survive (although popular myth puts it at twelve).

Following the battle and pursuit, Fidel and Raúl—along with the other revolutionaries—manage to reunite. Seeing Raúl and his comrades, Fidel exclaims: "Now we will win the war!" This expression at this particular moment causes Raúl to say with irony to René Rodríguez: "It seems that my brother has gone crazy." This famous story shows the enthusiasm Fidel always tries to instill in the revolutionaries, even in the most dramatic and desperate circumstances. Fidel knows that the morale of his fellow fighters is fundamental to winning any confrontation.

Political struggle and armed struggle

From boyhood, Fidel has read classics of military thinking, as many from Latin American history as from the history of the rest of the world. In the Cuban Revolutionary War, he tries to apply this knowledge from his youth. He also adopts the great conclusion of theorist Karl von Clausewitz (1780–1831), who avowed: "War is nothing more than the continuation of politics by other means." Armed conflict must be guided by a revolutionary political strategy. Military strategy should be approached from a political perspective (and not the reverse).

> Revolutionaries must have a strategy that combines political struggle with the military.

> War is the continuation of politics by other means. The political always leads.

Fidel with Vo Nguyen Giap

Fidel conceives of revolutionary struggle, even in its political-military phase, as a struggle of the masses. After the attack on Moncada, while still in prison, he writes to the two women who had fought with him: "Remember that at this moment, propaganda is vital; without propaganda there is no mass movement, and without a mass movement, no revolution is possible" (Letter to Melba Hernández and Haydée Santamaría, June 18, 1954). The next day, another letter continues: "Our immediate task is to mobilize public opinion in our favor ... we have the right to win the faith of the people, without which, I repeat a thousand times, revolution is not possible" (Letter of June 19, 1954). Anyone who accuses Fidel and Che of being "militants," "Foquists," or of otherwise subordinating politics to war, displays his or her extreme ignorance.

Cuban Revolution = Foquist Militarism?

Some years after Fidel's victory, when writing the history of the Cuban Revolutionary War, writers try to reduce it to a simple and false diagram on a blackboard. The revolution had been the product of four bearded young men who, isolated from the people, without a political agenda, and exclusively by shooting, had come from the mountains and imposed their ideas on an ignorant and passive people. This simplistic, deformed, and one-sided version does not correspond to what really happened in the 1959 Cuban Revolution.

No revolution can happen outside of the political struggle of the masses, even when power is taken through armed combat. In Cuba, in addition to forming the Rebel Army—whose commander in chief is Fidel Castro—the revolutionaries deploy for a complete political battle. They fight in the country and in the cities, in the "sierra" and in the "llano," with the guerrillas, the unions, the student centers. Between 1956 and 1957, an urban civic resistance movement is created in Santiago de Cuba. In addition, there are the clandestine actions led by Frank País García, chief of the urban militias of the July 26th Movement, those of his successor René Ramos "Daniel" Latour (1932–58) in Oriente, Faustino Pérez (1920–92) in Havana, and José Antonio Echeverría, student leader of the Revolutionary Directory (DR): four significant examples of the active urban struggle that accompanies the rural struggle in the Sierra Maestra.

I don't know why they always caricature us. The Cuban revolution doesn't only consist of a rural struggle.

We fight on all fronts: in the country and the mountains, in the cities, in the factories. In the neighborhoods, in the universities...

The Cuban Revolutionary War

From the end of 1956 through all of 1957, Fidel's troops succeed in getting through the first stage of the fight—survival against a powerful enemy—and the Rebel Army consolidates its core base of power and begins to grow. The first guerrilla front having been secured, on March 10, 1958, the second front is assembled and placed under the command of Raúl Castro while Che Guevara commands Column 8, the "Ciro Redondo." The invasion of the entire country—for which Fidel gives the orders to Che and Camilo Cienfuegos—begins with around eight hundred rebels, once the Rebel Army secures weapons and munitions from the official army of the dictatorship. In the twenty-five months of the Revolutionary War, rural battles are accompanied by urban battles in a strategy where Fidel, heading a command that unites the political and the military, combines the struggles of peasants with worker's struggles, the civic struggles of the middle classes, and student struggles. In April of 1958, entrenched throughout the country, the July 26th Movement calls a general strike, which fails. Before the end of the strike, Batista launches an offensive against the revolutionaries: he deploys five battalions to the Pico Turquino, seat of the rebel command, to strike the "definitive blow." The official army gathers nearly ten thousand men. But six months after defeating Batista's attack against the Sierra Maestra, the rebels already have eight guerrilla fronts and twenty-two columns. The rebels initiate a siege of the most militarily important parts of the country. Che Guevara begins the celebrated battle of Santa Clara with three hundred rebels against the three thousand soldiers concentrated in the city, who later receive reinforcements by armored train. Throughout the war, Batista's air force restocks its supply of bombs and munitions many times from the North American base at Caimanera—Guantánamo.

The world during the Cuban struggle

While Fidel's revolution is unfolding in Cuba, the rest of the world is living in the Cold War. Having defeated the Nazis and the Fascists in 1945, the two superpowers that divide "spheres of influence" are the US and the Soviet Union. During those years, the social order of the postwar period is consolidated on a worldwide level. In the developing West—ruled by the US—capitalism neutralizes rebel workers with bureaucratic unions and relatively "high" salaries. Monopolies can pay those salaries thanks to the exploitation of the Third World, where neo-colonialism has spread—it grants the ex-colonies formal independence, combined with a revamped and subtle pillaging of their economies. Internally, the US applies McCarthyism, combining repression of all dissent with spying, censorship and the oppression of its own citizens.

The social order of postwar capitalism has its counterpart in the Soviet Union—the blood-soaked country that loses twenty million people in defeating the Nazi invasion. During the postwar period in the USSR, a small, privileged group forms—the Stalinist bureaucracy—which, in isolation from the working people, pursues the internal persecution and repression of its own revolutionaries. With Stalin's death in 1953, another section of the Soviet bureaucracy takes control and promotes "peaceful coexistence" with imperialism. In Latin America, the USSR and its supporters oppose themselves to any armed struggle.

Quiet, boys! It's not the time for revolutions... the important thing is to maintain peaceful coexistence.

The Cuban revolution—a gift from the USSR?

Although in the twenty-first century it is only a memory, for a long time the supporters of the USSR will claim that the Cuban revolution succeeded only thanks to the USSR. They will forget that in those days, the USSR discouraged revolutions in the West and was opposed to all armed struggle, defending the theory of a supposed—and non-existent—"peaceful transition" to socialism.

We carried out the Cuban revolution! Nobody gave us anything. That's why, after the fall of the USSR, we remain on our feet with dignity.

The rebel army and the July 26th Movement do not rely on Soviet weapons, money, or advisors. They triumph over Batista's military dictatorship—and Batista's North American masters—with their own strength.

Revolution or "reason of state"?

It's inappropriate to confuse internationalism with "reasons of state." Revolutionaries from any country can easily express solidarity with other states where the workers have triumphed without having to follow their "advice" to the letter, nor to subordinate themselves to the circumstantial interests or political necessities that those states may have.

The Cuban people carried out the revolution! We didn't follow the "advice" or the directives of any nation.

Che in Sierra Maestra.

It's not necessary to ascribe our own revolution or our internationalism to "realism" or to the joint necessities of other nations. It's more the case that we have the same goals as the other nations do.

Lessons of the Cuban Revolutionary War

Beyond its many stories—humorous, unique, and unrepeatable—the Cuban revolution provides lessons with relevance to social movements, both in Latin America and in the world at large, even today.

Among these lessons: (a) Domination by the powerful, even military domination, is never absolute. Victory is possible! (b) To win, revolutionary unity is indispensable: respect each other's differences, but treat as more important that which unites people. (c) In marginalized, dependent countries, combine the fight for national liberation with the fight for socialism; not two separate revolutions at once, but one that combines both tasks. (d) In Latin America one must fight—at the same time—against imperialism, its local agents, and the native bourgeoisie. (e) All anti-communism is reactionary. (f) One must think for oneself, prioritizing the unsolved problems of one's own country. (g) One must think of politics as an ethical and moral project. Without morals, no struggle, war, or revolution can be won.

Che, Fidel's fighter

Already in his first battle, descending from the *Granma*, Ernesto Guevara is obliged to choose between a knapsack of medicine and a box of bullets. This represents a clear choice between being a medic or a guerrilla in the rebel army. He chooses the latter. From that point on he distinguishes himself as a fighter and a leader—and eventually he will become one of the principal commanders of the revolution, and the revolution's symbol on the world stage.

THE REVOLUTION HEADED BY FIDEL OFFERS POLITICAL LESSONS ON A GLOBAL LEVEL. THE FUNDAMENTAL PROBLEM OF THE REVOLUTION IS POWER. NO ARMY IS INVINCIBLE IF THE PEOPLE ARE PREPARED TO CONFRONT IT.

The actions, moral example, and thinking of Che Guevara have a special gravity and an important similarity to Fidel Castro's. Che, through his own meditations, develops an original vision and interpretation of Marxism that will be recognized around the world. Notwithstanding this, he always presents himself as Fidel's fighter. Even in his greatest writing, he refers to Fidel as the principal leader of the revolution. In *Socialism and Man in Cuba*—without a doubt his most accomplished work—he describes Fidel's leadership and charisma as a "Telluric force." The same can be found in his letter of departure, where he confesses to Fidel that if he is to die fighting under a different sky, his last thought will be of Fidel.

Camilo Cienfuegos

Although Fidel is the principal leader of the Cuban Revolutionary War, he does not fight alone. Real revolutionaries have nothing to do with Hollywood movies, where the protagonist is always a solitary "superhero" who fights alone. In addition to relying on Che, Fidel is accompanied by great fighters from the people. Among many others, the figure of Camilo Cienfuegos (1932–59) stands out: member of the *Granma* expedition, fighter in Che Guevara's column, later the commander of Column 2, "Antonio Maceo," and one of the major leaders of the revolution.

After the victory of the revolution, on October 28, 1959, a small plane that carries Camilo from Camagüey to Havana is lost at sea. By then Camilo is the chief of staff for the Rebel Army. US intelligence reports will spread a thousand slanders about his death: "Camilo was murdered," "'disappeared' by his rivals," etc. The CIA will repeat this strategy when Che goes to fight secretly in the Congo.

Raúl Castro and Barbarroja

From a very young age—having already grown up on Marxist readings—Raúl Castro has shared his older brother Fidel's militancy. He supports student protests, participates in the attacks on the courthouse and the Moncada barracks, is imprisoned, exiles himself to Mexico, becomes the co-founder of the July 26th Movement, goes with the *Granma* expedition and, after rising to the rank of commander in February of 1958, commands the eastern front (the "Frank País") of the Rebel Army. After the victory, Raúl is one of the heads of the Revolutionary Armed Forces (FAR), which defends the revolution against threats, hostilities, sabotage, and attacks by the most powerful empire on earth, the United States of America.

In the column led by Raúl, a young redhead distinguishes himself: Manuel Piñeiro Losada (1933–98), alias the "Gallego" (Galician), who much later will be Commander Barbarroja. This young Cuban had studied at Columbia University in New York. Before the revolution takes power, Barbarroja is in charge of the revolution's intelligence. After the revolution's victory, he is responsible for the security of the new revolutionary state as the minister of the interior and as the vice-minister of technology, and also as the director-general of national liberation and as the head of the American department of the Communist Party. In all of these positions, he is in charge of coordinating and supporting insurrections in many countries in Latin America and around the world. His legendary figure—ferociously hated by the CIA—is symbolic, representing Cuba's internationalism and support for all the revolutionaries and rebels of the world.

José Antonio Echevarría

Although in 1953 some university students view the secret activities that the young Fidel Castro takes against the military dictatorship with suspicion or misgivings, José Antonio Echevarría (1932–57) always maintains an open attitude. Setting aside personal animosity and not feeling jealous, he comports himself as a loyal companion and brother, and he commits himself to the struggle. As president of the FEU, he stands up for an amnesty for the Moncada prisoners. Toward the end of 1955 he forms the Revolutionary Directory, and in August 1956, he and Fidel sign the "Pact of Mexico," the first step towards uniting the revolutionaries against Batista.

> Comrade Fidel: the students will also fight against the dictatorship. All revolutionaries must unite!

On March 13, 1957, a group of young people from the Revolutionary Directory, led by José Antonio Echevarría, attacks the presidential palace and manages to get inside. Their objective is to bring Batista to justice. Another contingent from the same group captures the station Radio Reloj and broadcasts news about the battles. Batista manages to escape. The attack fails; a second revolutionary group does not give it the support it promised. The young Echevarría dies in action, but in the end manages to inspire an anti-dictatorial feeling within the people and—most importantly—among the young. From then on, his organization calls itself the Revolutionary Directory of March 13th.

Frank País and the urban struggle

Shortly after the death of José Antonio Echevarría on July 30, 1957, another young figure of the revolution is murdered by the dictatorship: Frank País García (1934–57), also known as David or Carlos. He dies along with his friend Raúl Pujols (1918–57). The deaths of Echevarría and País show the commitment of a young generation that gives everything, absolutely everything, to free Cuba from North American control, and from their local stooges: the prostituted native bourgeoisie of Cuba.

Like many members of the July 26th Movement's urban struggle—Armando Hart Dávalos (b.1930), Faustino Pérez, René Ramos Latour, and others—Frank País begins in the National Revolutionary Movement (MNR) and the National Revolutionary Action (ANR). There he fights in the open before joining the July 26th Movement, where he eventually becomes the national head of sabotage. This young student—who had enrolled in a teachers' college and presided over the student council—represents one of the greatest figures in this often-underestimated aspect of the Cuban Revolutionary War: the secret urban struggle in the big cities, carried out by "el llano."

Revolutionary women

Celia Sánchez & Haydeé Santamaría

That women took part in the Cuban Revolutionary War is not widely known, but fundamental when evaluating Fidel's actions. Once, when visiting Santiago de Cuba to provide humanitarian aid to the wives of the revolutionaries, the North American Ambassador Smith is surprised: the wives, as will happen much later in Argentina with the mothers of the Plaza de Mayo and with many others in Latin America, demand that the US stop giving aid to the dictatorship, remove all US assassins from the city, and end the murder of their sons. Yet the active, military role of women in the revolutionary war can not be reduced to solidarity, to the role of "mothers of" or "wives of." Many women participate directly as combatants and as guerrillas.

In addition to the famous Haydée Santamaría Cuadrado and Melba Hernández Rodríguez del Rey—both heroes of the Moncada assault—and to Vilma Lucila Espín Guillois (1930–2007), leader, with Frank País, of the November 11, 1957, uprising in Santiago de Cuba in support of the *Granma* landing and a guerrilla soldier of the eastern front of the Rebel Army (and later the wife of Raúl Castro), many female revolutionaries participate in the life of secret insurrection. In fact, in addition to guerrilla combat, they organize themselves into the all-female battalion "María Grajales," founded by Celia Sánchez Manduley (1920–80), who had been in charge of distributing Fidel's petition, *History Will Absolve Me*, in addition to being a co-founder of the July 26th Movement and a participant in the urban struggle. After the triumph of the revolution, the women will inspire the formation of the aggressive Federation of Cuban Mothers (FMC), whose first president is Vilma Espín.

Women are for pro-creation and cooking. They have nothing to do in a revolution.

67

Fidel and the media

Contradicting the official stories regularly sent out by the Batista dictatorship (reports of Fidel's death, for example), on February 24, 1957, *The New York Times* publishes a front-page article with photos of the rebels gathered in the Sierra Maestra and Pico Turquino. The photos are taken with a small camera belonging to Frank País. The interview is done by the journalist Herbert Matthews. Already, in this time of secrecy and guerrilla warfare, Fidel Castro clearly knows the fundamental role the media plays in class warfare and in the battle for public opinion.

Trying to create propaganda for a large public audience, the July 26th Movement, on February 23, 1958, symbolically kidnaps the Argentinean auto businessman Juan Manuel Fangio, which causes immediate repercussions. Fangio publicly acknowledges that he is well treated.

Our struggle for the conscience of the people will inolve every outlet of the media.

Herbert Matthews interviewing Fidel

In 1958, Fidel and Che offer interviews to the Argentinean journalist Jorge Ricardo Massetti on radio station El Mundo in Argentina. That same year, Che creates in the Sierra Maestra the revolution's own media outlet, Radio Rebelde, which begins transmitting on February 5. The bulletin *Patria*, media organ of the Rebel Army in las Villas, *Milicianos*, and *Revolución* all commence publication in 1958 as well. Much later, *Verde Olivo* is created.

The unity of the revolutionaries

Fidel understands that unity between the many revolutionary groups is indispensable—in Cuba and in any other place—to achieving victory. The enemies of the revolution try to sow discord, envy, and rivalry among those who wish to change society. "Divide and Conquer" is the slogan of the imperialists and the bourgeoisie who stir up fears of communism, equating it with "terrorism," "subversion," and "extremist groups"

The most difficult thing is unity. No revolution triumphs if revolutionaries insult and hurt one another. But listen: we must unite ourselves with those who fight... never with those in power!

In Cuba, the July 26th Movement secures the support of the Revolutionary Directory led by Echevarría, who signs the "Pact of Mexico" with Fidel on August 29, 1956, promising mutual support for the insurrectionist struggle. Shortly before the revolution's success, in June of 1958, Carlos Rafael Rodríguez interviews Fidel in the Sierra Maestra: the July 26th Movement secures the support of the PSP. Once in power, the three groups come together—under Fidel's leadership—to form the Integrated Revolutionary Organizations (ORI), the germ of the Union Party

The weapons of revolutionaries should never be used to hurt one another, but instead to fight against power, its institutions, its injustices, and its crimes.

José Carlos Mariátegui

of the Socialist Revolution (PURS) and the embryo of the new Cuban Communist Party (PCC) of 1965. Fidel predicts unity: "We have made a revolution larger than ourselves and each one of our organizations. We must unite, and bring our revolution to its highest point." (Speech of March 26, 1964)

Victory and arrival in Havana

On December 24, 1958, Batista's General Eulogio Cantillo asks for a meeting with Fidel to put an end to the hostilities. The meeting takes place at 8 a.m. on the morning of December 28. The military proposes an "orderly retreat" for the dictator. Fidel does not accept. On December 31, Cantillo executes a coup d'état that facilitates Batista's escape to Santo Domingo on January 1, 1959. He has the support of the US Ambassador Earl T. Smith, who is looking to frustrate the revolutionaries' triumph. The CIA (under Allen Dulles) and Francisco Tabernilla, commander of the Army, try other tactics as well.

There's no true revolution unless the people take power! Pretending to change society without trying to take power (not only the government's power) in the majority of cases is naïve.

Meanwhile, Fidel remains in Central America, coordinating the final takeover of Santiago de Cuba, where he receives news of Batista's flight. He gives the order to march on Havana and take the capital. By radio, Fidel broadcasts his famous quote: "Revolution, YES, coup d'état with Batista, NO." Moncada is taken without firing a shot after twenty-five months of revolutionary war. Fidel calls for a general strike of the entire island to support the Rebel Army. He accomplishes it easily. The rebel divisions take Santiago de Cuba and fight tooth and nail in Santa Clara and Havana until Fidel enters the capital on January 8, 1959. Contrary to all the rules of geopolitics (which declared it impossible for any nation to achieve victory as close as Cuba is to the United States), the Cuban Revolutionary War is over: the revolution succeeds.

The bourgoisie fails to co-opt the revolution

With the triumph of the revolution, Judge Manuel Urrutia Lleó (1901–81) is named president on January 5, 1959, and the politically anti-Batista José Miró Cardona (1902–74) is named prime minister, although the power remains effectively in Fidel's hands. Miró Cardona is discharged from his duties on February 13, 1959; Fidel becomes the prime minister. This produces a crisis in the newborn cabinet—which still contains traditional bourgeois politicians—due to the radical direction of the new government. Fidel renounces the office of prime minister under pressure, appealing to the masses. The people move to support him. On July 17, 1959, Urrutia, an anti-communist who is discontented with the government's agricultural reforms and radical methods, resigns and leaves for the US. He is replaced as president by the minister of law, the attorney Osvaldo Dorticós Torrado (1919–83). Fidel returns as prime minister.

This is what I don't understand about capitalism... normal? Capitalism is capitalism! So many sacrificed... our 20,000 martyrs didn't give their lives to continue with more of the same.

The crux of the dispute that polarizes the victorious opposition to Batista centers on the first revolutionary measures pushed through by Fidel: the reduction of rents (by 50 percent), housing programs, a reduction in the price of medicine, the forgiving of debts due to bad investments, and the prosecution of torturers and oppressors. In addition, on May 17, 1959, Fidel passes the first Law of Agricultural Reform: individual landowners can hold a maximum of one thousand acres, and the remaining property titles will be distributed to the peasants. This is too much for the traditional anti-Batista politicians! Disturbed by the shadow of communism, they want to replace one government with another, yet leave everything the same as before: to change something so that nothing changes. This happens all the time in Latin America.

Fidel travels to the US

Faced with the radicalization of the new Cuban government, the US State Department begins a campaign of misinformation. To counter it, Fidel travels to the US on April 15, 1959. President Dwight D. Eisenhower, who had been on good terms with the dictator Fulgencio Batista, declines to receive Fidel. The first thing Fidel declares: "I do not come for money." On September 26, 1960, Fidel makes a second trip to the US to participate in the 15th General Assembly of the United Nations.

The US government that opposes the Cuban revolution—in the name of "democracy" and "open society"—is the same which, in its sad history, oversees the trial and execution of the laborers Sacco and Vanzetti from 1920 to 1927 and that of Julius and Ethel Rosenberg in 1953, as well as the imprisonment of journalist and black militant Mumia Abu-Jamal for twenty-five years. It is a totalitarianism whose zenith is McCarthyism, the model for Ronald Reagan's "conservative revolution" in the 1980s and the "War on Terror" by George W. Bush, a totalitarianism whose rule is marked by long decades of surveillance, control, espionage, persecution, witch hunts, imprisonments, the neutralization, destruction and repression of all radical dissidents, manipulation of the popular will, election fraud (with the ascension of George W. Bush), and the predominance of large war-profiteering businesses that promote aggression and war throughout the world.

In Harlem with Malcolm X

When the Cuban delegation arrives in the US, the large New York hotels close their doors. In contrast, the black community opens them in admiration. Fidel Castro stays for ten days in the Theresa Hotel in Harlem. Here, Fidel meets with one of the principal leaders of the North American working class: Malcolm X (who had become a revolutionary while in prison). Malcolm is part of the "welcoming committee" that greets Fidel in Harlem and, in addition, guarantees his safety.

Fidel Castro and the Cuban revolution support the black protest movement in the US, in which several ideas coexist, ranging from the pacifism of Dr. Martin Luther King, Jr. to the radicalism of Malcolm X, who advocates the liberation of blacks "by whatever means necessary." During this time, Malcolm X adheres to the ideas of the "Nation of Islam," although at the end of his life his view broadens into a vision of global anti-capitalism. Not coincidentally, in "the country of liberty and diversity," both King and Malcolm X are assassinated.

Cuba in the North American black movement

From its beginning, the Cuban revolution maintains a close relationship with North American radical movements and their major intellectuals and political leaders, especially those which advocate "Black Power."

Beyond the initial link with Malcolm X, Fidel Castro supports many groups, including the Black Panthers. When Stokely Carmichael, one of the principal leaders of the Black Panthers, becomes the FBI's most wanted man in the United States, he travels to Havana (where he participates in the Conference of the Latin American Organization of Solidarity). Also, with a helping hand from Cuba, Carmichael travels to Africa to make political contacts. (There he stays in Guinea and Tanzania.)

We support the Black Panthers. We never defend terrorism. We support resistance and revolutionary struggle, which is not the same.

Barbarroja

Fidel reads Marx's *Das Kapital*

In 1960, in the middle of social radicalization, Fidel and the core leaders of the counsel of ministers study Marx's *Das Kapital* at a seminar. The professor who coordinates the group at the Presidential Palace is the Hispano-Soviet economist Anastasio Mansilla. Che participates, along with Carlos Rafael Rodríguez (1913–97, a member of the old PSP), Regino Botti (of the Central Planning Committee, who had studied at Harvard), and three other ministers. They read the translation by Wenceslao Roces from the Economic Culture Foundation. Although Fidel already studied Marx in his youth, this systematic seminar consolidates and refines his theoretical thinking even more.

> Hey, Fidel! You've done well to study economics, but don't forget that revolutions are also built on the grounds of culture, subjectivity, and ethics.

> Don't worry, teacher, remember that I'm also a follower of Martí.

According to the testimony given by Orlando Borrego Díaz (b. 1936, a member of the Rebel Army with Che and his principal assistant in the Ministry of Industry), the *Das Kapital* seminar is very animated. Professor Mansilla recognizes that his two most argumentative students are Fidel and Che. On one occasion Fidel tells Mansilla: "Professor, there is an error in the translation of the second book of *Das Kapital*." Mansilla responds: "No, Commander, you are mistaken. I have studied *Das Kapital* for years and I assure you there is no error." Fidel leaves. Later he returns and insists. Mansilla repeats that there is no error, but at home that night while reading, he notices it. He recounts that Fidel is most satisfied.

Democracy in Cuba

Defying everyone, Fidel Castro declares: "We gave the people more than the vote: we gave them rifles" (Speech of March 28, 1960). From August 22 to 29, 1960, the Organization of American States (OAS) condemns Cuba. The US thus brings in the rest of the OAS members against the Cuban revolution. As a response, on September 16, 1960, Fidel reads the "First Declaration of Havana" in the Plaza of the Revolution. With a strong, anti-imperialist tone, Fidel defines what he means by democracy. Revolution is not merely the overthrowing of a tyrant or a simple change in government. With massive popular assemblies—which continue for nearly fifty years—a new type of relationship has begun, much more democratic and fluid, between government and those governed.

In Cuba there is no democracy. We have to blockade it, isolate it, and invade it.

What better democracy than a people assembled, mobilized, and armed? We give rifles to the people. Does it cheer up the Latin American politicians to arm the people? Does it cheer up the servants of the United States to submit themselves to massive assemblies?

BUT YOU HAVE FIDEL! THE YANKEES CAN'T DEAL WITH YOU!

The nucleus of the "First Declaration of Havana" defends the democratic sovereignty of Cuba. Fidel identifies "democratic sovereignty" as the will of the people expressed in assembly. Calling it a direct form of representation, Fidel puts forward for a vote—in front of a million people—the anti-imperialist radicalization of the revolution. No other government on the continent is inspired to imitate him. In his speech, he defines the concept of "the people" as a union of workers, peasants, and students, excluding the so-called "national bourgeoisie" and local business owners. Shortly afterward, Fidel puts to rest the strategy Northern workers followed in class warfare: "The first duty of the working class must be to seize political power" (Speech of December 14, 1960).

The US offensive against Cuba and the revolution

US President Eisenhower begins his attack on the new Cuban government by lowering the quota of sugar Cuba can sell to the United States. In March of 1960, the US Security Council increases its measures by beginning a program of economic sanctions. Shortly thereafter, it suspends the sugar quota indefinitely, the precursor to the economic blockade that continues—like a spasm, one periodically reinforced and aggravated—to this day. The US also seeks to provoke an energy crisis: it orders refineries not to process crude oil sent by the Cuban government (crude oil that for the most part is provided by the USSR).

The large North American media monopolies of (mis)communication denounce, indignantly, the justice proceedings against Batista's torturers. Curiously, when these torturers remain free and unpunished—as happens in the majority of Latin American dictatorships—this same media is neither indignant nor offended.

America for the Americans! Castro wants to rebel? But who'll believe it? Cuba is our whorehouse and nobody'll stop us from amusing ourselves.

When the Cuban Revolution triumphed, they shot torturers and rapists. They can't admit it! And individual liberties?

In Miami: first money, then "nationality"

Faced with the ascent of the revolution, the Cuban bourgeois prefer to renounce their citizenship rather than lose their riches. For this reason, as in the rest of Latin America, the bourgeoisie can be called "native," but never "national"—even though they may like to play dominoes or listen to *danzón* or *salsa*, like other Cubans. When they flee to Miami, they take over $400 million with them, all stolen from the country.

In this way, they submit peacefully to the culture of the cruel master of the North, "who despises us and humiliates us." This brutal cultural submission has left its mark on the Cuban community in Miami even today.

Florida as a continental symbol

Until 1958—in pre-revolutionary Cuba—the largest group of immigrants to the US came from Mexico. Cuba was in second place. In 2004, Cuba occupies eighth place. When the large (mis)communication monopolies in the US show the arrival of Cuban emigrants in Miami, they "forget" to mention the Cuban Refugee Adjustment Act. This law guarantees that all Cubans who arrive in the US from January 1, 1959, to the present have legal status. (If they arrived before the revolution, they remain illegal.) Any Cuban who emigrates for economic reasons transforms artificially into a "political refugee." Compared to any other Latin American nationality—Brazilian, Argentinean, Chilean, etc., including the majority of undocumented Mexicans and Haitians—Cuban immigrants receive deferential treatment. The US wants to force emigration from the island. From 1959 on, Yankee administrators manipulate the problem of Cuban immigration without ever considering the flesh and blood immigrants. Everything is reduced to a problem of "national security" (read: a military strategy against the revolution and against socialism).

-Work faster, good-for-nothing Negro.

-In Miami they humiliate me and I'm far from my homeland. But I earn good money.

Cuban migration to the United States

There is a brutal economic disparity between the powerful United States and Latin American countries. As a result of economic dependencies, pillaging, and unequal trade, the US has come to dominate the entire continent. Because of this, tens of thousands of Latin Americans emigrate to the US. Mexico is the most common source of immigrants, but others come from Puerto Rico, Haiti, the Dominican Republic, Brazil, Argentina, and other Central and South American countries. These emigrants do not hate their countries of origin; they are looking for a better economic situation. Why would it be different in Cuba's case? One difference is that the US government calls Mexicans, Haitians, Puerto Ricans, or people from whichever Latin American country "immigrants," while Cubans are all "political refugees" and "enemies of socialism."

In Cuba, there have been various US migration crises: El Puerto de Camarioca in 1965 (300,000 emigrants), the Mariel Boatlift in 1980 (100,000 emigrants), and, in the 1990s, the *balseros*, or boat people (no numbers available, but far fewer than the previous ones). Cuba is not against anyone leaving the country if the destination country grants the immigrant a corresponding legal visa—something the United States does not do unless the emigrant throws himself or herself into the ocean on a rubber raft or small boat, or unless he or she hijacks a ship at knifepoint. Although the Cuban government periodically solicits visas from the US, very few are granted, which promotes illegal emigration. This creates a big splash in the media and serves as propaganda against the Cuban revolution.

In the US I have a car, a DVD player, and expensive shoes... how strange that the people in Havana are so happy.

Generations of Cuban emigrants

The Cuban emigrants who leave for the US are not all the same. The first generation in 1965 is made up of the Cuban bourgeoisie—Batista sympathizers, white and wealthy—who mostly leave for political reasons. Later generations are very different. The 1980 generation is made up of delinquents and lowlifes (masterfully depicted in the 1983 movie *Scarface*, directed by Brian de Palma, written by Oliver Stone, and starring Al Pacino). The 1990s generation of emigrants, made up of

highly educated people who seek better employment and higher living standards than Cuba can offer, leaves for economic reasons.

In his book-length interview with Ignacio Ramonet in 2006, Fidel Castro states: "More than 90% of those who emigrate don't have political agendas; they do it for economic reasons, like the Mexicans. Nor is it because they are uneducated, unhealthy, or starving... If they wish to emigrate, Cuba opens the doors for them, but the US closes them, only accepting illegal emigration from Cuba. If neo-liberalism promotes the free circulation of money, I defend the free circulation of people. The US should accept Cuban emigration by legal means! They should repeal the Cuban Refugee Adjustment Act! If there were a law of Mexican adjustment, what would happen?" The Cuban Refugee Adjustment Act, adopted in 1965 and still enforced, modifies the legal status of Cuban immigrants to that of political refugees, with the automatic right of asylum, the right to work, and a permanent resident card to live in the US. It looks better to accept an immigrant on a raft, filmed by CNN, than to accept a normal immigrant with proper documentation!

Torture and human rights

This is not a cry for vengeance for my tortured and murdered comrades. No one can put a price on their valor. The lives of all the criminals put together couldn't pay for them. The only worthy price is the happiness of our people.

The end of impunity

Torture is one of the worst crimes in the world. It takes the humanity away from a human being and places him lower than animals (who do not torture, who at most kill in order to eat). Torture not only destroys its subject, violating his or her human rights. It also marks the torturer himself with a stain that can not be erased. In the Middle Ages, torture was used by the Catholic Inquisition. Nearer to our times, the Nazis used it against "inferior people." England exercised it in Ireland and France in Algeria. The North Americans—heirs of the Nazis, English, and French—developed the use of torture in Vietnam and, by means of military dictators, throughout Latin America. (As of 2006, they continue torturing in Iraq, on the Yankee base at Guantánamo, and in other places…)

At least in my country the revolutionaries didn't win. They'd have judged us and shot us, just like in Fidel Castro's Cuba.

There is no worse insult to dignity, justice, and human rights than torturers enjoying impunity. Today, in all of Latin America, torturers—military officers and policemen trained by the Yankees in the School of the Americas and the Western Hemisphere Institute for Security Cooperation, as well as at West Point (according to *The Secret History of a Dictator: Trujillo*, by Victor A. Peña Rivera, published in 1977 by Mateu Cromo)—brag about their achievements: the rape of pregnant women, the torture of defenseless prisoners, the hundreds of thousands of the "disappeared." The only country in the entire continent that has succeeded in bringing these violators of human rights to justice is Cuba. Article 12 of the Rebel Army's penal code, ratified in the Sierra Maestra on February 21, 1958, establishes: "The crimes of murder, treason, espionage and rape will be punished on pain of death." With the victory of the revolution in 1959, torturers are judged by the people and sentenced. Their repressive apparatus is dismantled on January 8, 1959.

Human rights and torture

The US military adopts the torture techniques of the French (who used them in Algeria). Then, the US exports torture to Vietnam and to all of Latin America. Despite this, the United States press has a different agenda to talk about. They repeat: "Cuba tortures." Speaking out against the large media monopolies of United States (mis)communication, Fidel points out: "It doesn't matter what our enemies say. What they say are barbarities. We won't pay attention. You read any cable news outlet and they are irritated, furious, because in reality, they can't present a single scrap of evidence that the revolution has tortured anyone, or that a single person has been made to 'disappear'" (Interview with the Brazilian Dominican friar Father Betto, Havana, 1987).

While the American continent has suffered political repression and kidnappings, and while people have been made to "disappear," disappearances do not exist in Cuba. The French writer Regis Debray, a friend of Cuba in the past but now a sworn enemy, writes: "One must realize that Revolutionary Cuba is the only country that has never tortured" (R. Debray: *Praise Be Our Fathers*). Fidel affirms: "The phenomenon of disappearances is one of the cruelest things ever conceived of. This method is used on a massive scale by the tyrants imposed on Latin America by the United States" (Dialogue with unionists, Havana, July 18, 1987). In a previous speech, Fidel raised pointed questions: "I ask you, who taught these practices to those governments? Who trained the torturers in Argentina, in Chile, in Paraguay, in Brazil, in Guatemala, and in Colombia? Who trained them if not the United States?" (Discussion at the closing of the Study of the Woman's Situation in Latin America and the Caribbean, Havana, June 7, 1987).

CNN News: There is suspicion that in Cuba, human rights are being violated and people are being tortured...

Yes, there is torture... at the US base at Guantánamo! That's the only part of the island where people are tortured!

Danny Glover

Fidel's counteroffensive

Against this pressure from North America, Cuba reacts by improving its political process and radicalizing its social transformation. For example, faced with the US refusal to process crude oil, Cuba responds by putting foreign refineries (Texaco, Esso, Shell, etc.) under Cuban administrative control. Among the North American companies whose assets are nationalized are the Cuban Electric Company, the Cuban Telephone Company, and the United Fruit Company, among many others.

> For every Yankee reprisal we'll expropriate a business. They won't frighten us.

> History shows that if a revolution doesn't become more profound, it falls behind and crumbles. Compromises won't help.

When, in August of 1960—at the assembly of the First Latin American Congress of Students—Fidel announces these nationalizations and mentions the name, in English, of each company, the public shouts the phrase *se llamaba*, or "It *was* named..." Cuba offers a reasonable compensation package for each company, but the US does not accept. Celebrating, the Cuban people organize the mock burial of the North American companies.

Agricultural reform

When, on May 17, 1959, Fidel puts forth the first Law of Agricultural Reform from La Plata (a secret place in the Sierra Maestra where the Rebel Army took its first steps toward radical politics), he crashes head-on into bourgeois opposition. But in contrast to traditional Latin American politicians—who usually back down when they encounter stumbling blocks—Fidel speeds forward, and is supported by the masses.

On July 26, 1959, when the First Law of Agricultural Reform is made public, he brings together half a million peasants in Havana. The hidden Cuba, the Cuba of rustics, illiteracy and rural poverty, erupts in the capital. The political effect is devastating. Class warfare ignites and the revolution moves forward, declaring the year 1960 the "Year of Agricultural Reform."

In Cuba, to touch the great agricultural properties means getting involved with the Yankees. They're large landowners. Agricultural reform is woven together with anti-imperialism.

Literacy campaign

The literacy campaign is inaugurated in 1961. It faces the problem of over one million illiterates, nearly a sixth of the population. This is part of the heavy legacy of the capitalist regime, dependent and neocolonial, from before 1959. The literacy campaign is headed up by Armando Hart Dávalos (b.1930), one of the founders of the July 26th Movement and the minister of education from 1959 to 1965. The campaign begins in the poorest regions, where 100,000 young students enroll in the Literacy Brigades called "Conrado Benítez," named for a volunteer teacher murdered by counterrevolutionary groups that year in the mountains of the Escambray.

The Pedagogy of the Oppressed and popular education learned much from the Cuban literacy campaign.

Paulo Freire

Castro is crazy! To spend $$ on education is to squander it. The population should remain ignorant so it will be obedient and submissive. A notebook and a pencil are very dangerous weapons.

On December 22, 1961, Fidel proclaims from the Plaza of the Revolution that Cuba is a "land free from illiteracy." The campaign will later be taken as an example by many literacy campaigns on the continent, and will be influential, to some degree, on the thinking of Paulo Freire (1921–97), the father of the *Pedagogy of the Oppressed*.

"The revolution doesn't tell you to believe; it tells you to read"

The central idea of the literacy campaign is the link between revolution and reading, the synthesis of an entirely new vision of a world centered on critical thinking and a new historical subjectivity.

Socialism or Death!

At the same time, the large-scale vaccination of children against polio, diptheria, tetanus and other infectious diseases begins. Along with these campaigns of education and health, in 1961 the Pioneers Union, an organization of preteen children, is created.

These people grant much importance to books, to education, and to culture. In Cuba I feel at home.

Ernest Hemingway

The CIA: world politics against the people

The men of the CIA are wonderful! Sweet, tender, agreeable, educated, and persuasive.

The Central Intelligence Agency (CIA) is founded in the US in 1947 during the Cold War. The CIA inherits from its predecessor, the Office of Strategic Services, the duties of espionage, destabilizing enemies, psychological operations, clandestine action, and the intervention by North America in the internal affairs of other countries. Between 1947 and the present it has never stopped growing. This endless army of agents acts as a gigantic police force of global repression that spends millions of dollars on spying, holding countries in check, buying consciences and promoting acts of terror against all "heretics" and "dissidents." First among these: Fidel Castro.

"The United States CIA said that it promoted freedom of expression. For this purpose, they recruited Nazis, manipulated democratic elections, dosed innocent people with LSD, opened the mail of thousands of citizens, overthrew governments, supported dictators, trained assassins and bought consciences. In the name of what? Not of civic virtue, but of empire." Thus concludes the brilliant study, *The CIA and the Cultural Cold War* by Francis Stonor Sounders (Barcelona: Debate, 2001). The study demonstrates that the CIA—obsessed with Cuba and with Fidel—doesn't merely murder, organize coups d'état, invade nations, and install military dictatorships around the world. It also exercises its domination over the culture and consciences, from Hollywood to writers' foundations, universities, journalists, and non-government organizations.

We must control, crush, or buy off dissident thought.

CENTRAL INTELLIGENCE AGENCY

CIA

The CIA and the Nazis

The CIA organizes many of the coups d'état in Latin America, from the invasion of Guatemala in 1954 to the 1973 coup d'état against Allende in Chile, from the 1976 coup of General Videla in Argentina to the counterrevolution in Nicaragua during the 1980s, and from the more than six hundred assassination attempts against Fidel Castro (using poison, LSD, cigars, bombs, and a thousand other artifices) to the attempts to overthrow Chavez in Venezuela. The CIA teaches torture to Latin American policemen and members of the army, who kidnap, rape, and murder in the name of "national security." Among their instructors in torture are ex-Nazis from Germany (for example, the criminal Klaus Barbie, member of the US Army Counter-Intelligence Corps and advisor to the Bolivian army) and the French who worked in Algeria. The worst Latin American torturers publicly acknowledge having "studied" their techniques in Yankee schools.

> After the Führer fell, I went to work for the CIA and as an advisor for Latin American armies.

Klaus Barbie

From the insurrection against Batista onward, the Cuban revolution must confront aggression, interference, psychological operations, and terrorism from the CIA under Allen Dulles and other repressive organizations of US imperialism (such as the thirty-three intelligence agencies the US operates in 2006). On January 13, 1960, Dulles presents the "Cuban Project" to a special group within the Yankee government that begins to plan both the political and physical elimination of Fidel. The US breaks off diplomatic relations with Cuba: on January 3, 1961, more than three hundred North American diplomats—many of them spies—leave Havana. Due to the morbid obsession within the business elites and military of the US for control of both the hemisphere and the world, they must regard the Cuban socialist revolution as an affront. For half a century, the CIA will not stop trying to organize terrorist acts against the island.

North American terrorism against Cuba

In October of 1959, a traitor to the Rebel Army bombs Havana (killing forty-seven victims) using a plane that takes off from Florida. At the end of 1959, small planes coming from the US set fire to sugar plantations. On March 4, 1960, a violent act of sabotage occurs: there are strange explosions on the deck of the French ship *La Coubre*, carrying arms for the FAR from Belgium. This terrorist attack by the CIA leaves 101 dead and more than 200 injured. (After this North American sabotage, Cuba decides to buy arms from whoever will sell them: this establishes a relationship with the USSR and other Eastern Bloc countries.) There continues to be a succession of bombs and terrorist acts against both state and civilian targets in Cuba, including schools. Everything is part of the so-called "plan of covert action against the Castro regime"—authentic state terrorism—implemented by the National Security Council of the US.

> We must prevent the example of Cuba from spreading to other countries. We need to destroy this bearded one called Fidel Castro.

> Our agents on the island say that the people love him too much. The only solution is to assassinate him.

During the funeral services for the victims of the attack on *La Coubre*, Fidel pronounces for the first time the slogan: "*Patria o Muerte!*" (Homeland or Death!) Meanwhile, in the mountains of Escambray, former deputies of Batista, fortified with weapons and money from the US, organize a guerilla counterrevolution. They carry out acts of sabotage, arson, bombings, and murders (for example, they hang the volunteer teacher Conrado Benítez, who is teaching people to read in the mountains). They try to prepare the way for a future invasion. They are considered "bandits" by the people. They end by being destroyed and dismantled by the FAR in the operation called the *Limpia* (cleaning) of Escambray.

The Latin American response to the CIA

Before 1959, the revolutionary forces were laying the groundwork for their security and intelligence operations. With the triumph of the revolution, these become the Ministry of the Interior and the Vice-Ministry of Technology, headed by Manuel Piñeiro Losada, alias "el Gallego," or, more popularly, "Barbarroja." The "Buró de Atentados" (Bureau of Criminal Transgressions) is born, a special unit charged with investigating CIA plots, acts of sabotage, and conspiracies designed to eliminate Fidel Castro, Guevara, and other revolutionary leaders. Some members of the Bureau are Mario Morales Mesa, alias "Miguel" or "Maxim" (a veteran internationalist fighter in the Spanish Civil War), Carlos Enrique Díaz Camacho, alias "Trillo," José Veiga Peña, alias "Coco" or "Morán", Carlos Valdés, Pedro Piñeiro, and Fabián Escalante Font, among many others.

To defend ourselves against the CIA, we'll organize our own intelligence and security services; then we'll be able to help revolutionaries in Latin America, Africa and Asia.

Barbarroja

In addition to these intelligence organizations designed to watch for and to counteract CIA terrorism in Cuba, Fidel creates the General Department of National Liberation (DGLN), which years later will be named the American Department of the Communist Party. Its task is to coordinate and support insurrections in Latin America and the world. (Section 5 is dedicated to African rebellions.) Together with these organizations, in October of 1959 the National Revolutionary Militia (MNR) and the Committee for Defense of the Revolution (CDR) are also created. Camilo Cienfuegos then declares: "We are not afraid of the masses; that is why we distribute weapons to the people."

Worldwide revolution

In contrast to the majority of Latin American governments that habitually give in to US pressure—in the name of "the possible" and "realism"—the Cuban leadership reasons: "The Yankees persecute us? We will take them on in every corner of the world, especially in Latin America, Africa, and Asia." With this in mind, facing a crowded Plaza, Fidel pronounces his celebrated slogan: "The backbone of the Andes will be the Sierra Maestra of Latin America" (Speech in the Plaza of the Revolution, July 7, 1960). This plan brings together at the same time: (a) the historical continuity of San Martín and Bolívar's projects for continental independence, and (b) the internationalism of the Cuban revolution.

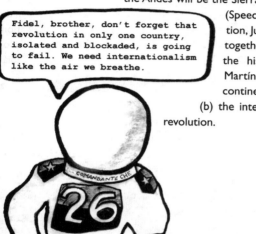

Fidel, brother, don't forget that revolution in only one country, isolated and blockaded, is going to fail. We need internationalism like the air we breathe.

I totally agree, Ernesto! Our project is continental and our battlefield contains the entire world.

Based on this, Fidel asserts: "We know that our liberty will never be complete and honest while other people are not as free as we are; we know that in our struggle against imperialism we will never be able to come out victorious if we do not support the efforts of all those who fight against imperialism. Therefore, our battlefield embraces the world" (Speech in the Cuban Workers' Headquarters, August 29, 1966).

Support for revolutionary Latin American movements

The Latin American right wing—quoting pamphlets from the US—have insisted that "Fidel Castro and Cuba intend to export revolution." This point of view presupposes: (a) that people are by nature passive (only rebelling if an "outside influence" appears), and (b) that the Cuban revolution is an exceptional and isolated event, unusual in the history of America. On the contrary, history demonstrates that from the beginning, Latin American rebellions have

Long live the Latin American socialist revolution!

always been and continue to be continental projects. From the indigenous rebellion by Túpac Amaru to the revolutions for independence by San Martín and Bolívar, all rebellions embrace many different nations and lands. Fidel affirms: "Revolutions are not exported; the people make them!" (Speech of February 4, 1962).

Carlos Fonseca   Roque Dalton   Miguel Enríquez   Raúl Sendic   Mario Roberto Santucho

Conceiving of Cuba as "the first free land in America," Fidel thinks of the revolution as a continental project. They are not "exporting" anything—with the exception of their example. Cuba is simply a chapter in the greater struggle that encompasses all of Latin America. It is from this that all rebels have found comfort, collaboration, and support on the island: the Revolutionary Workers Party-Revolutionary Army of the People (PRT-ERP) of Argentina, the Movement of the Revolutionary Left (MIR) of Chile, Tupamaros (MLN-T) of Uruguay and the ELN of Bolivia, the MIR, PRV, and FLN of Venezuela, the FMLN of El Salvador, the FSLN of Nicaragua, and many others.

Kennedy, the CIA, and the Bay of Pigs invasion

Shortly after the rupture of diplomatic relations between the US and Cuba—more precisely, on April 15, 1961, at 6:00 a.m.—the airports of Santiago de Cuba, Ciudad Libertad, and San Antonio de los Baños are bombed. It is the prelude to the mercenary invasion of Playa Girón (or the Bay of Pigs), the largest military operation organized by the CIA. It happens during the Kennedy administration.

Although imperialism now wears sheep's clothing, it continues to be imperialism. We will resist the mercenary invasion organized by the CIA. We will not let ourselves be humiliated. We will defend our socialist revolution to the end.
To arms! Homeland or death!

The invasion fleet sets off from Somoza-controlled Nicaragua. The dictator Luis Somoza, puppet of the North American political machine in Central America, shouts at the fleet at the moment of departure: "Bring me a lock of hair from the beard of Castro!" The assault brigade consists of seven battalions, made up of fifteen hundred men enlisted in Miami, sixteen combat planes, five Sherman tanks, ten armored cars, and twenty-one recoil rifles. The brigade has more firepower than the entire Rebel Army had while fighting Batista. Its first victims are civilians.

We will defend our socialist revolution to the end.
To arms! Homeland or death!

The transition to socialism begins

On the day after the first bombardment of Cuban airports, during the burial of the victims on April 16, 1961, Fidel declares the socialist nature of the revolution. The transition to socialism begins.

> In this plaza and before these people I declare the socialist character of the revolution. We will conquer!

In total, the CIA's counterrevolutionary adventure leaves 176 Cubans dead and more than 300 wounded. The CIA planes are marked with the initials of the Cuban army as a distraction. The invasion—which attempts to establish a beachhead to allow direct intervention from the US—is defeated in less than 72 hours. The last mercenary position is overrun at 5:30 p.m. on April 19. It is Playa Girón: the first great defeat for imperialism in Latin America. Cuba takes 1,197 mercenaries as prisoners (many are former property owners, the sons of plantation owners, members of high society, and Batista's torturers). The US agrees to pay a ransom for the mercenaries, giving Cuba indemnification costs of $62 million. The prisoners are exchanged for medicine and food. The exchange becomes known as "mercenaries for preserves."

> They have firm principles. They synthesize anti-imperialism and socialism, focusing on ethics and culture... yes, sir! I like the Cuban revolution!

Two revolutions, or the same process?

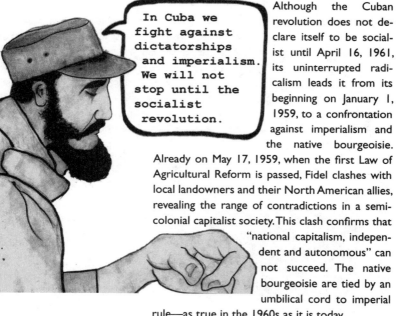

In Cuba we fight against dictatorships and imperialism. We will not stop until the socialist revolution.

Although the Cuban revolution does not declare itself to be socialist until April 16, 1961, its uninterrupted radicalism leads it from its beginning on January 1, 1959, to a confrontation against imperialism and the native bourgeoisie. Already on May 17, 1959, when the first Law of Agricultural Reform is passed, Fidel clashes with local landowners and their North American allies, revealing the range of contradictions in a semi-colonial capitalist society. This clash confirms that "national capitalism, independent and autonomous" can not succeed. The native bourgeoisie are tied by an umbilical cord to imperial rule—as true in the 1960s as it is today.

The revolution begins with a radical social program of national emancipation. Then, almost immediately, it marches toward socialism. Finding the balance, Fidel explains: "The revolution had to be anti-imperialist and socialist. Anti-imperialist and socialist revolutions need to be the same, a single revolution, because there *is* only one revolution. That is the great dialectic truth of humanity: imperialism, and against imperialism, socialism" (Speech on Cuban television, December 1, 1961).

The Latin American socialist revolution will be one phase of the world revolution. To the word "socialist" we will add the adjectives we want: anti-imperialist, agrarian, nationalist, revolutionary. Socialism supposes these, predates these, and embraces all of these.

Carlos Mariátegui

Playa Girón and moral strength

How was the victory at Playa Girón possible? In May of 1961, Che Guevara tries to explain it this way: "The North Americans made mathematical calculations, as if they were faced with the German army and were coming to establish a beach-head in Normandy: 'this many Germans, this much firepower, we pour this many men in, we take the beachhead; we put land mines here, organize everything, and already we're all set.' Perfectly organized, with the efficiency they have in matters like this. *But they forgot to measure the moral strength of our forces.* They badly underestimated our capacity to react when faced with aggression, our capacity to mobilize our forces and to send them to the battlefield. *They badly underestimated our ability to fight.*"

Che continues: "They calculated that one thousand men were sufficient to face any resistance—but they needed one thousand men willing to fight to the death. Then we would have been on equal ground, but with a high cost in terms of lives, because the operation, from a military point of view, was well-conceived. But one can't order a man whose father had a thousand acres of land—a man who returns to Cuba just to be ceremonially present so that the thousand acres will be returned to him—to go and kill: to come face-to-face with a peasant who has nothing and who wants, with a barbaric fury, to kill this person who came to steal that peasant's land. This is the part that machines don't know how to measure. This is how they could be so greatly, so fantastically mistaken."

Kennedy and the CIA defeated at Playa Girón

The Organization of American States does not condemn the Bay of Pigs invasion, and as a result Fidel names them: "the Ministry of Yankee Colonies and Military Blockades Against the Latin American People" (Speech of February 5, 1962). Straining the limits of impudence, the US proposes expelling Cuba from the OAS. After the defeat at Playa Girón, Robert McNamara, the US secretary of defense, reproaches the CIA for their ineptitude. He then creates another intelligence service, one answerable to the US Department of Defense: the Defense Intelligence Agency (DIA), which will be added to the Bureau of Intelligence and Research within the US State Department, geometrically multiplying the US's capability to police the entire world.

Following their shameful defeat, the Yankees implement "Operation Mongoose," which consists of shooting at the Cuban coastline—hurting and killing civilians—from artillery ships coming from the US. Robert Kennedy, the US president's brother and attorney general, summarizes his goals in the following way: "My idea is to stir things up on the island with espionage, sabotage and general disorder, run and operated by Cubans themselves…" In 1992, Robert McNamara and Arthur Schlesinger (both secretaries of defense for Kennedy and Johnson, respectively) publicly confess that "Operation Mongoose" consisted of "creating an internal revolt in Cuba." In February of 1962, the economic, financial, and commercial blockade against the island is decreed.

Second Declaration of Havana

On January 25, 1962, Cuba is expelled from the OAS by the US and its puppets, with the exception of Mexico. At an assembly in the Plaza of the Revolution, Fidel responds with the Second Declaration of Havana, a manifesto that outlines the history of Latin America—including the domination by Spanish colonialism and Yankee imperialism—from the perspective of the working classes and subjugated people: "those who by their work accumulate the riches, create values, and make the wheels of history move forward, and who today wake up from the long, stultifying nightmare that has subjugated them."

> Humanity has said "ENOUGH!", and its forward march will not be stopped. No one will die uselessly now, not even in service far away. If anyone dies, it will be as it was at Playa Girón: for their true independence.

In this speech/manifesto, anti-imperialism is combined with a socialist identity, and the idea of the "national bourgeoisie" is questioned: "In the actual historical conditions of Latin America, the 'national' bourgeoisie can not lead an anti-feudal and anti-imperialist struggle. The experience shows that in our nations this class, even when faced with the contradictions of imperialism, has been incapable of opposing it, paralyzed by fear of social revolution and of the exploited masses..." (Speech of February 4, 1962). Che agrees with Fidel: "The native bourgeoisie have entirely lost their capacity to oppose imperialism—if they ever had it—and are only the caboose on imperialism's train. There are no more changes to be made: either socialist revolution, or the caricature of a revolution" (Che Guevara, "Message to the People of the World from the Tricontinental").

North American attacks on Cuba

During the first four years of the revolution, Cuba suffers more than four hundred attacks and acts of sabotage, perpetuated by the CIA and its Cuban agents. For example, Eduardo Ferrer, ex-pilot for the CIA, revealed publicly that between September 1960 and March 1961, the CIA carried out sixty-eight aerial missions to supply weapons and explosives to counterrevolutionary bands on the island (*Operation Puma: The Aerial Battle of the Bay of Pigs*, 1982). Even though it succeeded in thwarting the Bay of Pigs invasion, Cuba is blockaded economically by the US.

Luis Posada Carriles. Terrorist following the orders of the CIA.

For years, the CIA persists in its terrorist acts against Cuba (despite the US rhetorical condemnation of terrorism). In 1976 the CIA—acting as the Godfather to Orlando Bosch, Luis Posada Carriles, Hernán Ricardo, and Freddy Lugo, among other terrorists from Miami's extreme right—succeed in bringing down a Cuban civilian plane in flight over Barbados. They murder seventy-three passengers and crew. That same year, anti-Castro terrorists detonate a bomb in Jamaica, in a mail bag carried by a Cuban civilian plane. They also attack Cuban civilian passenger boats. These and other terrorists from Miami—José Basulto, José Hernández Calvo, José Dionisio Suárez Esquivel, Gustavo Samper, and Félix Rodríguez—murder Chilean economist and activist Orlando Letelier in Washington, DC, participate in the dirty war in Nicaragua, and collaborate closely with the military dictatorships in the southern part of Latin America (Videla, Pinochet, Stroessner, etc.)

The Cuban Missile Crisis

As a result of the permanent aggression of the US against Cuba—as much from the Bay of Pigs invasion as from as the cannonades of "Operation Mongoose"—the Cuban Missile Crisis arrives. To defend itself against new aggressive acts, Cuba signs an accord with the Soviet Union to install medium-range ballistic missiles on the island. Cuba proposes to make the agreement public. The Soviets refuse. The US threatens the island with a nuclear holocaust. On October 22, 1962, the crisis explodes. The US demands that the USSR remove the missiles and forms a naval blockade of Cuba. The next morning, Fidel puts his forces on alert. On October 27, Cuba shoots down a U-2 spy plane that flies over its territory. The world reaches the brink of nuclear war.

Kennedy and Khrushchev negotiate about missiles... but no one consulted the people of Cuba!

After six days of the crisis, on October 28, Fidel Castro and the Cuban leadership learn of the settlement between Kennedy and Khrushchev. Cuba presents a five-point demand to the United States: the end of the blockade, the end of aggression through invasions, spies, and sabotage, the end to piratical attacks and the shelling of its coastlines, the end of airspace violations, and the return to Cuba of the naval base at Guantánamo. But the Soviet leadership is more worried about the North American missiles in Turkey than about the sovereignty of Cuba.

The Kennedy assassination

On November 22, 1963, while traveling in an open car in Dallas, Texas, President Kennedy is killed by several gun shots to the head and neck. Although the US officially blames Lee Harvey Oswald (who is "curiously" murdered two days later by the Dallas night club owner Jack Ruby), many believe that the CIA is behind the assassination, conspiring with the Mafia and Cuban exiles who are upset with Kennedy's "soft hand."

Miami's extreme right and the most anti-communist factions in Washington want to implicate Fidel Castro for the assassination of Kennedy, but the Warren Commission of the US Congress—placed in charge of investigating the assassination—comes to the conclusion that Fidel and the Cuban government have nothing to do with it. Many years later, in 1991, the North American movie director Oliver Stone makes the celebrated film *JFK* and places responsibility for the assassination on the CIA and the anti-Castro Mafia of Miami.

The complicated support of the USSR

The link between Cuba and the USSR does not begin with the missile crisis, but rather much earlier. As the US increases its pressure and aggression against the newborn revolution, the Soviet Union offers major economic and military support. One of the first Soviet diplomats to visit Cuba is USSR Vice-Premier Anastas Mikoyan, a man steeped in the subject of economic relations.

The Yankees want to crush us. We want to be independent, but we need support to oppose this world power. Still, I worry about the USSR, China, and other eastern countries...

Raúl and Che

CUBA

Don't worry about them any more, Fidel. This alliance will help us to speed up our transition to socialism and to promote world revolution.

Defying US threats, Mikoyan is received in Havana as a "guest of honor." Among other exchanges, Cuba begins to sell sugar and nickel to the Soviet Union in exchange for petroleum. This link benefits the revolutionary government in Havana, which maintains, despite the USSR, total independence in ideological and political matters. Cuba does not formally join the Council of Mutual Economic Assistance (CAME, an organization of Eastern European countries, founded in Moscow in January 1949) until thirteen years after the triumph of the revolution, in 1972.

The politics of the USSR in the 1960s

After the death of Stalin in 1953, supreme power in the USSR passes into the hands of Nikita Sergeyevich Khrushchev (1894–1971), first secretary of the Communist Party Central Committee from 1953 to 1964 and head of the government from 1958 to 1964. In 1956, Khrushchev heads the 20th Congress of the Central Committee, where he denounces—post mortem—the crimes of Stalin. He thus begins a "Stalinism without Stalin," a modernization of the elite bureaucracy that governs the USSR.

Cuba is useful in geostrategic terms. Enough with revolutions!

Nikita Khrushchev

We must maintain the political system that Stalin built, but with some changes. I will promote the free market in the USSR, as well as "peaceful coexistence" with the US.

In internal politics, Khrushchev promotes market reforms, mainly in the realm of agriculture. In international politics, he proposes the "peaceful coexistence" with capitalist imperialism, always based on respecting the "spheres of influence" formulated during the postwar period: the USSR in the East, the US in the West.

The USSR and revolutions in the Third World

In the 1960s, Khrushchev is the greatest proponent of the doctrine of a supposed "peaceful transition to socialism" (later attempted unsuccessfully in the 1970s by Salvador Allende in Chile and by European communists in Italy, France, and Spain). This is why the USSR does not support insurrections or revolutions in Latin America and the Third World, especially those that develop into armed struggles. Cuba is no exception.

Soviet comrades: We need your help to fight against imperialism in the Third World.

We'll give it to you...if you obey, and if it it supports our geo-strategy.

The USSR under Khrushchev supports Fidel Castro and his colleagues only after they triumph and take power, mainly due to Cuba's conflict with the US and its geo-strategic position in the West, but the Cuban Revolution prior to 1959 did not receive Soviet aid (nor did they ask for it). During the entire decade of the 1960s, Cuba and the USSR, although they collaborate, maintain divergent political lines: more radical in the case of Cuba, more moderate in the case of the USSR and its allied countries in Eastern Europe. In the 1960s, Khrushchev's politics generate conflict and an eventual break between the USSR and Mao Zedong's China.

Fidel vs. Lenin and Stalin

The Bolshevik Revolution in Russia succeeds in October of 1917. It is headed by Vladimir Illyich Ulyanov, alias Lenin (1870–1924), and aided by the founder of the Red Army, Leon Davidovich Bronstein, alias Trotsky (1879–1940). After the death of Lenin in 1924, the dispute between Stalin and Trotsky grows. Heading an elite and authoritative bureaucracy, Stalin monopolizes his power by eliminating— through show trials—almost the entire Bolshevik Central Committee of 1917. He rules from the 1930s to 1953. When he dies, he is succeeded by Khrushchev. During the prolonged relationship between Cuba and the USSR, Fidel declares himself a disciple of Lenin, a profound admirer of the Bolshevik Revolution, but a critic of Stalin.

- Fidel, what have the bureaucrats done with our Bolshevik revolution?
- Teacher, no sacrifice is wasted. We will pass on your rebellion to the young.

The Stalinist bureaucracy squandered the "assault on heaven" that was 1917, as well as the heroism of the Soviet people, who sacrificed 20 million people for the defeat of the Nazis. To explain Stalin and the Soviet bureaucracy, on April 18, 1992, Fidel says: "Stalin's worst errors were—in addition to his abuse of power, his cruelty, his purges, and the violation of law—the forced collectivization of his country, the unprincipled pact with the Nazis in 1940, the occupation of a part of Poland, the war with Finland, his poor leadership of the Soviet Army, not having mobilized his entire population against the Nazi invasion, and his overcautious reaction to that invasion." On September 4, 1995, Fidel elaborated: "Hitler continued to acquire power in Europe; the USSR continued a political purge in which it committed all variety of abuses and crimes. It practically beheaded the Party, and as for the armed forces, it completely stripped them of their leaders, contributing to the creation of the most adverse possible conditions when the moment for war arrived… had it not been for the tremendous errors by Stalin, World War II would have ended in Portugal, not in Berlin. The Red Army would have won in Europe and there would have been neither a second front nor the North American landing in Europe."

Cuba, the USSR, and ideological controversy

The differences between Cuba and the USSR—although they maintain an economic link and collaborate with one another—are not only political. They are also theoretical and ideological. The controversy centers on the nature of Marxism. In Fidel's thinking (as well as the thinking of the major leaders of the revolution, such as Che Guevara), ethics, free will, subjectivity, history, and values are taken as the basis of revolutionary theory, as opposed to the focus on economics, the gradual transition to socialism, the determinism, and the Eurocentrism found in the variety of Marxism consecrated as "official" in the old USSR.

Marxism is like the natural sciences: it has laws that you can't violate.

If a country hasn't developed its productive power, it isn't mature enough for socialism.

To have a revolution is anti-scientific craziness!

The originality of the theories of Fidel, Che, and the Cuban revolution brought a new reading—a noneconomic reading—to Marxism. Revolution is not only based on the economy; it also covers ethics, culture, a new subjectivity, and values. This Latin American contribution by Cuba to world thinking accords with other revolutionary perspectives from Europe, such as the "cultural" Marxism of Antonio Gramsci or the dialectical Marxism of György Lukács, Henry Lefebvre, and Karel Kosik, among many other heterodox thinkers.

This "science" is metaphysics. They push it and prod it in their minds, but one mustn't forget about the moral factors with which people have realized the great tasks from the history of humanity.

Fidel vs. the Stalinist bureaucracy

Faced with the North American giant and its nuclear power, Fidel accepts Soviet aid. Although they have differences, he believes that the collaboration between Cuba and the USSR—in matters regarding the military, the economy, energy policy, etc.—is indispensable to avoid surrendering Cuba "to the cruel Northern master who despises us and humiliates us." Nevertheless, Fidel warns from the beginning that he will not allow into the Cuban revolutionary government fanatics who will try to pass on the bureaucratic methods of the Soviet government to the island.

There are several anticommunist gestures within the July 26th Movement, such as the PSP's attempt to divide the revolutionary groups. Fidel's questioning of sectarianism and bureaucracy is repeated on several occasions. Among these: in July of 1961, when the group Integrated Revolutionary Organizations (ORI) forms, the PSP tries to take control of all bureaucratic positions. Later, in 1962, a conspiracy forms against Fidel and Che, headed by Aníbal Escalante, organizing secretary of the ORI, and a small Stalinist group that operates from a Soviet ship. Then there is the March 1964 trial of Marcos Rodríguez, an informer and a traitor during the Batista era, who is protected by two high-ranking members of the PSP. Supporting Fidel's critique, Che in 1963 writes the article "Against Bureaucracy." In his speeches on May 1, August 29, and September 28 of 1966, Fidel stresses the "servile mentality" created by Soviet dogmatism and its reliance on rote procedures and guidelines.

> Castro and Guevara don't understand that we are the leaders of world socialism. They're too rebellious! We need to replace them with someone more docile, who'll obey us. They try to think with their own minds. Heretics! Revisionists! Ultra-leftists! Romantics! Adventurers!

"Words to the Intellectuals"

Even as they repel North American attempts to destabilize the political process—attempts ranging from terrorism and invasions to nuclear threats—the revolution moves forward on its firmest grounds: culture. On June 30, 1961, in the National Library in Havana, Fidel gives a famous speech that will be remembered as the "Words to the Intellectuals." Some of the most renowned intellectuals and artists of Cuba are there: José Lezama Lima, Virgilio Piñera, Antón Arrufat, Julio García Espinosa, Santiago Álvarez, Tomás Gutiérrez Alea, Nicolás Guillén, Lisandro Otero, Carmelo González, Roberto Fernández Retamar, Guillermo Cabrera Infante, Carlos Franqui, Alejo Carpentier, and Alfredo Guevara, among many, many others.

> Culture is meant for the few. The people don't understand anything. The revolution doesn't bother me or distract me.

> Novels are only tools for teaching. The only things worth writing about or filming are muscle-bound workers. Everything else is trash!

> Neither aristocratic elitism nor cheap populism. A free culture and social revolution should grow together. Within the revolution everything, against the revolution nothing!

In contrast to what had happened in the Soviet Union in 1934—in the era in which Stalinism consolidated politically and imposed, as its "official doctrine" in aesthetics, the idea of socialist realism—in Cuba there is no official aesthetic. Many currents proliferate, many schools and artistic traditions, from the avant-garde to realism, from "magic realism" to formalism. In his "Words to the Intellectuals," Fidel makes it clear that the revolution is open and contains everything, as long as it is not counterrevolutionary.

Books for everyone

One of the first books that the revolution publishes is *Don Quixote* by Miguel Cervantes. The first printing is of one hundred thousand copies, sold at an absurdly low price. This edition marks a historic change of direction in Cuban political publishing. Starting in 1959, the Cuban National Press is headed by the celebrated writer Alejo Carpentier. Fidel creates "Ediciones R" (Revolutionary Editions) and the Institute of the Book, both subsidized by the state. These organizations pirate thousands of titles from around the world. Fidel declares publicly that Cuba will not ask for authors' permission for this, nor will Cuba pay them. Culture during the revolution should be free, should be subsidized, and should not be subordinated to the market.

We struggle against the windmills of capitalism and imperialism. Culture in the hands of the people is a dangerous weapon against the powerful!

This passionate cultural and publishing policy makes up an essential part of the entire ideological offensive with which Fidel stamps the revolution. As part of that offensive and that radicalization, an organization for young rebels changes itself into the Young Communists' Union (UJC). The adoption of communism on the part of the revolutionary youth reclaims the radical heritage of Julio Antonio Mella and the heroic communism of the 1920s. Their symbols are: study, labor, and the rifle. Che Guevara greets this ideological shift, encouraged by Fidel, with a celebrated speech known as "What Must A Young Communist Be?" (October 20, 1962).

Cinema of the revolution

In 1959, the Rebel Army's Department of Culture is created. They film the documentaries *Esta Tierra Nuestra* by Tomás "Titón" Gutiérrez Alea (1928–96) and *La Vivienda* by Julio García Espinosa (b. 1926). These become a part of the Cuban Institute of the Arts and Cinematographic Industry (ICAIC), created in March of 1959. Its president, Alfredo Guevara Valdés (b. 1925) announces the takeover of the Yankee film distribution companies. In addition to the movie studio, the seventh floor of the ICAIC building is the meeting place for many Latin American insurgents. The ICAIC promotes its own style of cinematography and holds debates at public meetings. Its movies premiere in film festivals around the world. With Santiago Alvarez, director of "The ICAIC Newsreel," the new Cuban documentary is born. In 1961 the "Cine-moviles"—traveling movie theaters—are created using trucks, motorboats, and mules.

In the "Cine de la Base," Cuba also showed us the way.
Raymundo Gleyzer
on the "Cine de la Base"

Titón directs many great movies, such as *Memorias del Subdesarrollo* and *Death of a Bureaucrat*. The ICAIC introduces the Sound Experimentation Group as well as the Graphics and Audiovisual Experimentation Group and Kinematics. In 1963, there is a controversy. The head of the ICAIC, Alfredo Guevara, has a dispute with Blas Roca, head of the old PSP, who opposes the showing in Cuba of Fellini's *La dolce vita*, *Accattone* by Pier Paolo Pasolini, *The Exterminating Angel* by Luis Buñuel, and *Alias Gardelito* by Lautaro Murúa. Twenty-nine Cuban filmmakers sign the document "Conclusions of a Filmmakers' Debate," opposing Roca's position, which is the same as that of the USSR. Together with *Casa de las Américas* and the National Ballet (headed by Alicia Alonso), the ICAIC does not give in to the restrictive Soviet criteria for movies that will proliferate in Cuba during the 1970s. In addition, the Foundation and the Festival for New Latin American Cinema and the International School of Cinema and Television are created in San Antonio de los Baños.

Casa de las Américas: cultural ambassador

Casa de las Américas is founded on April 28, 1959, by Haydée Santamaría Cuadrado, heroine of Moncada. After the blockade, when all of the governments of the continent—with the exception of Mexico—break off relations with Cuba under orders from the US, *Casa* becomes the cultural ambassador of the revolution. While spreading Cuban artistic works, *Casa* plays host during the visits to Cuba by many intellectuals and critics from Latin America and the world at large: Julio Cortázar, Roque Dalton, Haroldo Conti, Juan Gelman, Mario Benedetti, Gabriel García Márquez, David Viñas, the young Vargas Llosa, and Juan Rulfo, among many, many others.

The fundamental role of *Casa de las Américas* goes together with the place that culture and ethics hold in the Marxist thinking of Fidel, Che, and the revolutionary leadership: theirs is primarily an aesthetic and cultural Marxism. Moral strength and cultural warfare are neither a passive "reflection" of the economy nor a decorative adornment for politics (as they are in the Marxism practiced by the USSR and similar countries). In addition to promoting writers, fine artists, musicians, dramatists, and students of literature, the arts, and the social sciences,

> Casa de las Américas will be the cultural ambassador of the revolution. With culture we will break any blockade.

Haroldo Conti

Casa shelters intellectual heretics and iconoclasts. Haydée Santamaría protects and supports Silvio Rodríguez, Pablo Milanés, Amaury Pérez Vidal, Noel Incola, and Sara González: the founders of the "New Cuban Composition," which is often misunderstood by dogmatists. *Casa* also welcomes Wilfredo Lam (the painter of Afro-Cuban hybrid forms), the poets Cintio Vitier and Pablo Armando Fernández, and many others. After the death of Haydée Santamaría, Mariano Rodríguez (1912–90) is the head of *Casa* from 1980 to 1986, and after 1986, the poet and essayist Roberto Fernández Retyamar (b. 1930) takes over.

The Latin Press against (mis)communication

To counter the counterrevolutionary propaganda of the United Press and the Associated Press, and to support balance in the media, on June 9, 1959, in the Hotel Nacional in Havana, the Latin Press, the primary Latin American news agency, is created. The main force behind its creation is the Argentinean journalist—a close friend of Fidel and Che—Jorge Ricardo Masetti. García Márquez, and Plinio Mendoza will be Masetti's correspondents in Colombia, Mario Gil in Mexico, Díaz Rangel in Venezuela, Teddy Córdoba in Bolivia, Aroldo Wall in Brazil, García Lupo in Ecuador and Chile, Onetti in Uruguay, and Triveri in the US. Working together with Masetti in Havana was another Argentinean, Rodolfo Walsh. Jean-Paul Sartre and the North Americans Waldo Frank and Charles Wright Mills will be frequent collaborators.

Rodolfo Walsh

The news agencies and their monopolies manipulate the world's information. We must create our own news agency. Information is a weapon in the hands of the people!

Many years later, in the twenty-first century, Fidel Castro and Hugo Chávez of Venezuela attempt to make something analogous to the Latin Press by creating a new Latin American television channel: TELESUR. Today, more often than ever before, the fight against imperialism is decided in the realm of consciences, minds, and hearts. Faced with the global dictatorship of the great media monopolies of (mis)communication, cultural resistance and alternative journalism continue to be vital.

Freedom of speech in Cuba and the US

The big US television networks, which in a monopolistic way manipulate the information of North American citizens, repeat *ad nauseum* that "in Cuba, there is no freedom of speech." What do they mean by this? Simply that there are no pro-USA newspapers or TV broadcasts on the island (which does not mean that all Cuban newspapers are good; some are excellent and others are mediocre or bad; there is a little of everything). Faced with the absence of a pro-US press, many media powers in the United States can't think of anything better to do than to create illegal radio and TV broadcasts—violating Cuba's airspace—that emit anti-communist propaganda continuously, as happened during the Cold War, and that promote the "American Way of Life," as practiced by the US. This radio and TV (paradoxically calling itself "Martí," even though Martí was a virulent anti-imperialist) is financed, as even the *New York Times* has shown, with the support of the North American state.

The newspapers, publishers, and several other organizations and political parties—including those that are liberal and progressive—rarely ask themselves: Does real freedom of speech exist in the United States of America? Do the lower classes—the poor, workers, women, unions, and, most importantly, radical dissidents—have a *real chance* to influence public opinion via the mainstream media and the major television networks? The answer can be found in the excellent books by

Noam Chomsky. According to Chomsky, the US does not have freedom of speech, but rather "manufactured consent" on an enormous scale.

Fidel's political speeches

Fidel's political speeches—which sometimes last for hours—are celebrated. Fidel himself jokes about them, alluding to their incredible length. The speeches exemplify the continual dialogue he maintains with the masses, even in moments of great tension (as with the Cuban Missile Crisis or the many threats of North American invasion of the island.)

Tell me, Mr. Castro: Why is it that your speeches are so long? In our country, the United States, the presidents speak very little.

In a true democracy, the people must know what's being dealt with: "public matters" must be truly public. We believe in a politically-active population, and in an ongoing dialogue with the masses.

If Che Guevara is the great theoretical writer of the revolution, Fidel is, in addition to being the principal political strategist and charismatic leader, fundamentally the great orator. His speeches prioritize simple language and are always both didactic and educational. Fidel's major thinking can be found more often in his speeches than in his writings.

Ho Chi Minh and the Vietnamese revolution

Ho Chi Minh (1890–1969), whose real name is Nguyên That Thanh, is the supreme revolutionary leader in Vietnam. He heads the fight against colonialism and Japanese, French, and North American imperialism. In 1911, he works as a ship's cook. Later, he travels to London and Paris, where he participates in the founding of the French Communist Party. Uncle Ho, as the Vietnamese affectionately call him, discovers in Lenin an understanding of the colonial struggle and anti-imperialism: "The first time I read Lenin, it made me cry." Fidel and Che greatly admire Ho Chi Minh and learned from his example.

Following Lenin, Ho Chi Minh leads the Vietnamese against the Japanese invaders (1941–45); against the French colonialists (1945–54), who were defeated at Dien Bien Phu; and against the Yankee invaders in the 1960s, who are definitively defeated in 1975. (Uncle Ho dies in Hanoi in 1969.) Vietnam is united into a single socialist country. In the brutal war, the US kills four million Vietnamese, and leaves thousands burned by napalm—a true genocide!

Repercussions of Vietnam and Cuba on Europe and the US

The Vietnam War is responsible for the growing youth protest movement in the great cities of imperialism. From the hippies in the US to the 1968 student rebellions in Paris, Berlin, Rome, Tokyo, and London, the protests are marked by opposition to the imperialist genocide in Vietnam. Without the anti-imperialist struggles in the Third World—led in Asia by Vietnam, in Latin America by Cuba, and in Africa by Algeria—there would have been much less substance to the student revolts, countercultures, and youth rebellions of the developing capitalist world.

Cuba and Vietnam influenced the events of May 1968 in France and the youth revolts in the United States.

BE REALISTS: ASK FOR THE IMPOSSIBLE

The youth of the United States refuse to be drafted in the Yankee armed forces to go and kill the Vietnamese people on the other side of the world. This creates social unrest in North American society. In Europe, this unrest develops into student rebellions. If the most famous of these is May of 1968 in France—led by Daniel Cohn-Bendit, or "Danny the Red"—the most radical and meaningful is the rebellion in Germany. This is led by Alfred Willi Rudolf Dutschke (1940–79), known as Rudi Dutschke, a Marxist student who follows the teaching of Ho Chi Minh, Fidel Castro, and Che Guevara, along with the philosophy of Herbert Marcuse (1898–1979). Ulrike Meinhof (1934–76), from the German radical left, also came to prominence in 1968. Throughout 1968 in Europe, opposition to the war in Vietnam—and the influence of Cuba—help to determine the course of history.

Fidel and Cuba's support of Vietnam

Vietnam and Cuba establish diplomatic relations on December 2, 1960 (Vietnam opens its embassy in Havana in 1961). Although the Warsaw Pact does not include Vietnam within its sovereign territory, Fidel declares in 1965: "For Vietnam, we are ready to give our own blood... we must cut off the hands of the imperialists, in Vietnam or wherever we find them," while Che proposes to "create two, three, many Vietnams." Cuba offers to send volunteers (soldiers trained in anti-aircraft fighting) to Vietnam. Fidel travels to the country three times. In 1974, he visits the territory liberated from South Vietnam. He returns to the country in 1995, and makes his last trip in 2003 to meet with General Vo Nguyen Giap, minister of defense from 1945 to 1980 and legendary war hero in the Vietnamese victory against imperialism. (Giap's 1964 book, *War of the People, Army of the People,* includes a prologue written by Che Guevara.)

Strength, men! Those murderers are using napalm. But in both Cuba and Vietnam we'll defeat them.

In September of 1963, the Cuban Committee for Solidarity with Vietnam is created. Melba Hernández, heroine of Moncada, heads it. On December 20, 1963, Guevara speaks during the "Week of Solidarity with the People of South Vietnam." On February 13, 1969, Melba Hernández is received by Ho Chi Minh in Hanoi. In March of 1969, in the middle of open war, Cuba—also the first country to recognize the Viet Cong in July of 1962—establishes an embassy in the jungle, side by side with the revolutionary government in South Vietnam. In 1971, the first Cuban medical team arrives in Vietnam, where they remain for a year, attending to those wounded during North American napalm attacks. In 1974, in Dong Hoi, in the province of Quang Binh, recently liberated and still smelling like gunpowder—and before the liberation of Saigon—Fidel establishes the Vietnam-Cuba Friendship Hospital with 450 beds. That same year, Cuba organizes the Committee for Material Aid to Vietnam.

Vietnam, socialist power, and unequal trade

The Cuban revolutionary government, in solidarity with Vietnam, questions the insufficient aid provided to Vietnam by the USSR and China. In his "Message to the People of the Third World from the Tricontinental," Che maintains: "North American imperialism is guilty of aggression. We already know that! But those who balked at making Vietnam a sovereign part of the socialist world are guilty as well. And those who continue their war of insults and tricks: the two greatest powers in the socialist world. Is Vietnam isolated or not, while it maintains its balance between the two great powers in their conflict?" Fidel extends this criticism to those who send arms to Vietnam and the Third World, but who charge for this service: "We would never conceive of sending a bill to anyone for weapons that we give them, or of sending a bill for our technical advice; we wouldn't do it even if we did think of it" (Speech of August 23, 1968).

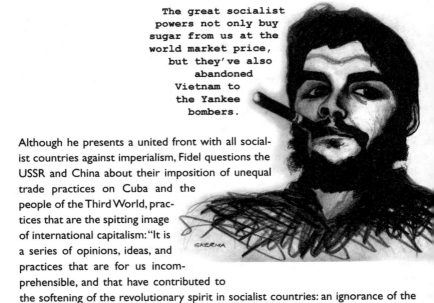

The great socialist powers not only buy sugar from us at the world market price, but they've also abandoned Vietnam to the Yankee bombers.

Although he presents a united front with all socialist countries against imperialism, Fidel questions the USSR and China about their imposition of unequal trade practices on Cuba and the people of the Third World, practices that are the spitting image of international capitalism: "It is a series of opinions, ideas, and practices that are for us incomprehensible, and that have contributed to the softening of the revolutionary spirit in socialist countries: an ignorance of the problems of the developing world and the misery that continues there, and a tendency to continue the business practices that the capitalist, bourgeois developed world uses against the developing world" (Speech of August 23, 1968).

Fidel and the revolutionary movement in the Third World

From its beginning, Fidel stamps the Cuban revolution with a multifaceted yet Third World-centric point of view. His policies in the Third World have three aspects, symbolized by the rifle, the teacher, and the doctor. Cuba sends weapons to all rebels who fight against the injustices of capitalism—the most well-known of Cuba's policies—but also sends thousands upon thousands of doctors, teachers, and other humanitarian aid workers to the most distant corners of the world that struggle against imperialism. Cuba funds hospitals, medical schools, and health centers in Vietnam, the Democratic People's Republic of Yemen, the Sahrawi Arab Democratic Republic, Niger, Gambia, Senegal, Honduras, Nicaragua, Venezuela, Tanzania, and countless other countries.

At the same time, Cuba welcomes to its Latin American School of Medical Science thousands of humble young men and women from all across Latin America who study, for free, in Havana. Together with this humanitarian aid, Fidel attempts to bring together an immense patchwork of countries that have been subjected to neocolonialism. For this work he will become, much later, one of the principal leaders in the Non-Aligned Movement (NAM).

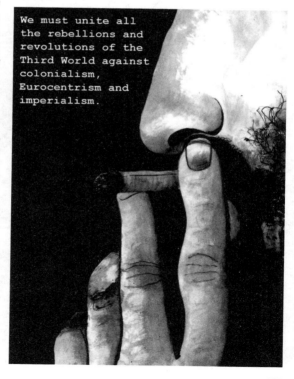

We must unite all the rebellions and revolutions of the Third World against colonialism, Eurocentrism and imperialism.

Fidel, Palestine, and the "Jewish Question"

In the Middle East, Fidel supports the Palestinian people, as led by the PLO. Some of his intelligence agents—in particular Ulises Estrada Lacalle, who works for Barbarroja—support the Palestinians during their guerrilla war on the West Bank. At the same time, Fidel gains the support of progressive Jewish organizations who are opposed to "Zionism." Just as there is a difference between the North American people and the elites who govern the US, so is there a difference between the Jewish people and the Zionist extreme right in both Israel and the US. (For example, in 2005, Communist Party intellectuals in Israel finish editing a book on Che Guevara in Hebrew.)

The Cuban Revolution supports the Palestinian cause against imperialism in the Middle East.

We, the anti-imperialist and socialist Jews of the world, also support our Palestinian brothers against Israel and the United States.

NOAM CHOMSKY

In Latin America, many groups—Jewish, anti-imperialist, and socialist—join the revolutionary struggle in support of Cuba and the Palestinians. Among many others, one of the founders of the National Liberation Movement/Tupáramos in Uruguay, Mauricio Rosencof (b.1933), is Jewish. The same is true in Argentina of the founder of the Revolutionary Armed Forces (FAR), Marcos Osatinsky (assassinated in 1975), and of Raymundo Gleyzer, the leader of the Workers' Revolutionary Party–People's Revolutionary Army (PRT-ERP) ("disappeared" in 1976). All of these are Latin American Jews, as well as anti-imperialists and followers of Fidel and Guevara.

Cuba and Algeria

In 1954, Ahmed ben Bella (b.1918) founds the National Liberation Front (NLF) of Algeria, which brings together both nationalists and Marxists. The NLF leads the insurrection against France in an eight-year war, until Algeria declares independence in 1962. French colonialists and settlers belonging to the Organisation Armée Secrète (OAS) kill a million Algerians and employ acts of torture and rape on a large scale, methods also implemented by their US disciples in Vietnam and Latin America. Colonel Huari Bumedián (1932–78), leader of the National Liberation Army, supports ben Bella, who is elected president in 1962. Algeria becomes a headquarters for African revolutionaries (in the same year, Nelson Mandela receives his guerrilla training there). But in 1965, Bumedián executes a coup d'état against ben Bella.

France tortured a million Algerians. The United States learned those methods and used them in Latin America. In contrast, Cuba and Fidel supported us.

Ahmed ben Bella

Fidel supports Algeria's struggle. His first act of aid in Africa is to send a boatload of weapons for the NLF, which arrives in 1961. That same boat returns with war orphans and wounded Algerians, who are treated in Cuba. The most fruitful period of Algerian-Cuban relations occurs during President ben Bella's administration. Under Bumedián, the relationship does not disappear, but becomes chillier. In addition to Algeria, Cuba supports the guerrilla warfare in Portuguese Guinea and in other African colonies like Angola and Guinea-Bisseau.

Fidel, Che, and the revolution in Africa

Although the aid to Algeria is the initial step, the Cuban revolution's presence in Africa continues today. Cubans lend assistance to the fighting in Angola, Zaire, the Congo (where Che fights), Ethiopia, the Western Sahara, Guinea-Bissau, and Namibia. Cuba does not only send humanitarian aid—doctors, teachers, and engineers—

Our people, before being free, were exploited as workers and slaves. The colonialists brought slaves from Africa to Cuba. Now we return to Africa to fight together with you for your independence and your liberty.

but also thousands of soldiers. The majority of these go to Angola: 450,000 Cubans total (380,000 soldiers and 70,000 civilians.) At the same time, 7,895 young Angolans study in Cuba. Angola trains, with Cuban help, 20,000 insurgent fighters from Namibia (from the Southwestern African People's Organization, founded in 1966), Zimbabwe, and South Africa (for the African National Congress, which fights against apartheid).

Agostinho Neto   Patrice Lumumba   Nelson Mandela   Amílcar Cabral

In 1977, at the first meeting of the People's Movement for Angolan Liberation, Raúl Castro announces: "And when Cubans leave Angola, we are not thinking about carrying off anything: oil, diamonds, coffee, nothing. We will only take with us the unbreakable friendship of this great people and the remains of our dead." Thanks to Cuban activities in Africa, in 1978 Namibia succeeds in gaining its independence from South Africa and white South Africans are forced to end their racist system of apartheid. From then on, in Namibia, South Africa, and Zimbabwe, the blacks, the majority of the population, begin to rule—the people who before this moment were reduced to living in ghettos as "inferior beings." Fidel and the Cuban revolution maintain total solidarity with Africa, a solidarity that has never before existed between a Western country and another country of the Third World.

Masetti and Che's Argentinean disciples

> The Cuban Revolution is continental. Our next step is Argentina.

Solidarity does not end with Africa. Cuba also aids revolutions in Latin America. On the day Fidel and Che meet, Che asks Fidel to allow him to return, after the victory in Cuba, to the revolution in Argentina. The first project Che takes on in Argentina is to work with the Guerilla Army of the People (EGP), an organization led by the journalist and founder of the Latin Press, Jorge Ricardo Masetti, who dies fighting in Salta, Argentina. Che considers joining a second group of the EGP to fight for socialist revolution in the southern regions of Latin America.

Before arriving in Salta—where Che's school friend Hermes Peña, who fought with him in Cuba, dies—Masetti's group goes to Algeria. The "Angelito" accompanies him: Alberto Bayo, the Spanish ex-colonel who trained Fidel and Che in Mexico. They make contact with Bumedián, head of the Algerian National Liberation Army. Later they travel through Bolivia—helped by Inti Peredo and Rodolfo Saldaña, who dies with Che in 1967—en route to Argentina. In Cuba, Masetti trained in the struggle against the counterrevolutionary groups in the Escambray. To this day, Masetti's body remains lost in the jungles of Salta.

> If we fail, other young people will take up the banner and learn from our example and our mistakes. In the people's memory, all those sacrificed will remain alive.

Jorge Ricardo Masetti

Fidel assigns economic duties to Che

Once the Cuban Revolutionary War has begun, but before the Rebel Army triumphs and takes power, the most difficult stage of the revolution begins: the creation of a new society, pursuing the strategic goals of socialist revolution and of the radical and permanent change of people, social relationships, and institutions.

We need someone to take charge of the National Bank. Is anyone here an economist?

Did I hear you say "communist?" Yes, I'm a communist, and I'll take charge of the National Bank.

Faced with the absence of people with technical knowledge—many of whom were terrified of the revolution, or who were counterrevolutionaries, and who escaped to Miami—Fidel appeals to the imagination and versatility of his revolutionary comrades. This is how Ernesto Guevara, a doctor by profession, is named by Fidel as the head of the Department of Industry at the National Institute of Agricultural Reform, and later as the president of the National Bank, and still later as the Minster of Industry.

The economic (and political) debate begins

Fidel is obsessed with maintaining the unity of the revolutionaries in the July 26th Movement, the DR 3/13, and the old PSP. At the same time as he names Guevara, a July 26th Movement member, as the head of the National Bank and as the minister of industry, he names Carlos Rafael Rodríguez, a PSP member, as the director of the INRA, a position Rodríguez holds from 1962 to 1965. Fidel offers the leadership of the economy to the Economic Commission of the national leadership of the Integrated Revolutionary Organizations (ORI), composed of Rodríguez, Osvaldo Dorticós, and Guevara. There, Rodríguez and Guevara debate about salary increases (meaning the role of material incentives), the leadership of the economy, city planning, and the primary system for financing companies. The Cubans Alberto Mora, Marcelo Fernández Font, Luís Alvárez Rom, Juan Infante, and Alexis Codina also participate, as do the Frenchman Charles Bettleheim and the Belgian Ernest Mandel.

In 1963, a public debate begins between Guevara and Rodríguez—both of whom studied *Das Kapital*, together with Fidel, under Anastasio Mansilla. The discussion, largely economic but also political, begins with practical problems: the measuring of production costs for business and agricultural products. Later, it divides into two economic, political, and philosophical camps. The debate is public and open; all of the positions taken are aired and published, and no one is persecuted or prohibited from speaking (as happened in debates in the USSR). "Inside the revolution, everything; outside the revolution, nothing," Fidel had said about the arts. This is also true for the social sciences.

The two basic philosophies of the debate

The Cuban political trends that come into play during the debates are (a) the political tradition of Carlos Rafael Rodríguez, who is a part of the Cuban revolution, an anti-imperialist, a defender of Fidel, and a critic of the counterrevolutionaries, but who wants to encourage the link between Cuba and the USSR, and (b) Che Guevara's position, also revolutionary and anti-imperialist, equally an adherent of Fidel's ideas, but which proposes the important step of autonomy—political, theoretical, and cultural—from the Soviet position.

To advance toward socialism, we need to industrialize and plan the economy, creating a communist conscience with moral incentives, and we need to centralize our financial resources.

CHE

To develop the country, we need support for the market, material incentives, and a decentralized economy. Each business must be profitable; if it isn't profitable, it's useless.

CARLOS RAFAEL RODRIGUEZ

The two foreigners involved in the debates also belong to well-defined political camps. Charles Bettelheim is a professor of political science from the Sorbonne and offers advice on city planning during the first years of the Cuban Revolution. He serves in the French Communist Party, which favors the Soviets, although he is also sympathetic to China. Ernest Mandel is another, equally famous European thinker and militant. He is an economist, a Jew from Belgium, who had been a prisoner of the Nazis and who escaped the concentration camps. He is the author of classic books and celebrated as a Marxist economist. Politically, he heads the Fourth International, which follows Trotsky's thinking.

The USSR's supporters during the debate

Che's principal opponents are Carlos Rafael Rodríguez and Charles Bettelheim. In 1930, Rodríguez belongs to the Student Directory, much later to the Left Student Wing, and, from 1936 on, to the PSP. For six months in 1944, he is a member of Batista's cabinet, following the policies that the USSR imposes on the Communist Party. Later, the PSP does not support either Fidel or the attack on Moncada. But, in the middle of the war, one section of the Party

Productive forces ALWAYS come first. The relationship between production and conscience ALWAYS develops afterward.

Charles Bettelheim

backs the revolution: in June of 1958, the PSP names Carlos Rafael as its delegate to Fidel in the Sierra Maestra.

Bettelheim is from the French Communist Party. In 1934, he learns Russian and in 1936 he travels to the USSR to study Stalin's economy. Although in the 1960s he is both pro-Soviet and pro-China, he never leaves behind his adherence to Stalin. Bettelheim, in line with Stalin thought, conceives of Marxism as "objective." Above all, he relies on the "general laws of the economy." He concludes that the law of values (which Marx termed the function of the market) must be followed to the letter. His basic philosophy, which Carlos Rafael shares, affirms that the transition to a socialist economy must be carefully managed over a long period of time. Each business that belongs to the people must conduct itself according to the goals of "self-sufficiency" and profitability. The businesses must not depend on any central agency, but on their own resources. They must maximize profits and minimize losses. Cuba does not have a developed economy, therefore it is not "mature" enough for socialism. This position taken by Bettelheim and Rodriguez follows to the letter the staged transition proposed by Stalin in his *Economic Problems of Socialism in the USSR* (1952). To motivate people to work—putting an end to absenteeism or reluctance—it is necessary to give material incentives.

As the USSR shows:

1. It's necessary to appeal to the market.

2. It's necessary to develop industrial capabilities.

3. It's necessary to offer monetary incentives.

4. Then, when there is material abundance, we can create socialism.

Che's Latin American Marxism in the debate

In disputing this, Che updates Mariátegui's critique of *etapismo*: conceiving of society and history as if they were ladders, impossible to climb by skipping steps. According to Guevara, although Cuba does not have a developed economy, it can move quickly toward socialism. The law of values—the market—is not absolute; it rules over all capitalist societies, but does not need to rule over the transition to socialism. Che asserts: "We do not feed the market; on the contrary, we try to destroy it in any way possible." In the transition to socialism, when there is a revolutionary leadership, the revolution can become involved—through economic planning—in the process of destroying the market. Socialist businesses should take social necessities as their guide, not earnings or profitability. They should not have their own money, but rather a single centralized bank account. They must create the goods that society needs, not those which bring them money.

We don't have to resign ourselves to the market. Although our industrial capacity may be weak, the communist conscience can accelerate transformation by means of economic planning.

How can a business motivate its workers if their efforts don't depend on the profits of the business, which then rewards them with material incentives? They must be motivated—Che believes—by appealing to their socialist consciences. The rewards must exist, but they must be primarily moral rewards: nothing more than achieving society's recognition for having carried out their social obligation of working for others. He who does this will be part of the vanguard of society. This "vanguard" will be made up of those who make the greatest efforts, who press forward, who go above and beyond when doing their duties, who give the best part of themselves to improve society and to help others. Workers will be motivated by morals, rather than money or material things. The grounds of the debate move from the market to the sphere of ethics. That's how a society can triumph over capitalism!

Two strategies for the Cuban revolution

Che: Both of us want the same thing. But our approaches are very different.

Carlos R. Rodríguez

The difference between the two positions in the Cuban debate is not only an economic difference, but also a political and philosophical one. The political argument concerns the course of the Cuban revolution: should it be socialist, but with the goal of Latin American autonomy? Or should it be guided by the directives of the USSR and its elite bureaucracy? The debate has philosophical implications. The two camps hold different understandings of Marxism.

The position of Carlos Rafael and Charles Bettelheim takes an evolutionary view of history, one in which revolutionaries must respect, almost religiously, each stage of development: If Cuba is less developed economically, how can it speed up the creation of a socialist state? It's impossible! In contrast, Che's position—supported by Mandel—presupposes a more dynamic, less mechanical view of history, where subjectivity and conscience are at work. In addition, it questions Eurocentrism: Although a country on the outskirts of Europe may be backward, that country doesn't need to cross its arms and wait until the "more advanced" free them. These points of view are condensed in his critical book, the *Manual of Political Economy*, from the Academy of Sciences in the USSR, published in Cuba in 2006 under the title *Critical Points of Political Economy*.

So be it. We have at heart different ideas on strategy for the Cuban revolution. Not only economic differences, but also political and philosophical ones.

Fidel's position in the debate

Although Fidel studies *Das Kapital* together with Che and Carlos Rafael (in Mansilla's seminars), his view of the debate is political. His obsession is to unite the different camps in order to guarantee that the revolution will continue, avoiding the disaster of the USSR after the death of Lenin (where groups would try to destroy, even to murder one another; practices which never take hold in Cuba). Fidel chooses an "intermediate solution," preserving the alliances between both camps and both of the traditions represented by Che and Carlos Rafael.

1 Trade is the basic component of capitalism. A "mercantile" socialism is craziness.
2 Economic relationships are a part of power relationships.
3 Taking into account both sides of the issue, one must strengthen oneself to achieve equilibrium in the Cuban debate and to guarantee the political unity of the revolution.

Nevertheless, while arriving at a stable equilibrium, Fidel agrees with Che's reasoning. "I have thought much about Che... Che was radically opposed to using and developing the laws and the economic systems of capitalism when building socialism; and he proposed something on which we have insisted many times: that the building of socialism and communism is not only a question of producing and distributing wealth, but also a question of education and conscience. I do not want to become a judge between the different theories, although I have my own ideas. I only ask, modestly, that the economic thinking of Che become known... There are many ideas of Che's that are absolutely, totally valid, ideas without which I am convinced that we will never be able to build communism" (Speech of October 8, 1987).

Fidel and the construction of political consensus

Fidel's leadership often finds itself at a crossroads similar to the one faced by Lenin. The Bolshevik leader was also faced with fiery controversies, and many times he had to opt not for his own positions—the most radical—but rather for compromise solutions in order to guarantee the allegiance of workers, peasants, and the majority of the revolution.

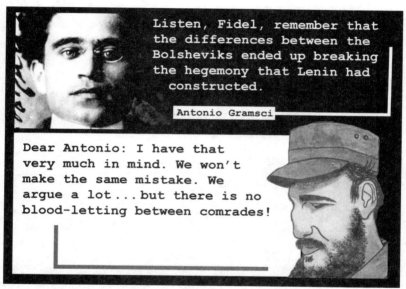

Listen, Fidel, remember that the differences between the Bolsheviks ended up breaking the hegemony that Lenin had constructed.

Antonio Gramsci

Dear Antonio: I have that very much in mind. We won't make the same mistake. We argue a lot ... but there is no blood-letting between comrades!

Fidel is faced with the same challenge of maintaining the revolution, rebuilding, day by day, the consensus of civil society and the unity of the different revolutionary groups against imperialism, and the example that unity sets for other rebel groups. Notwithstanding, though, that he takes consensus as more important than his personal opinions, Fidel inclines in the debate toward Che over Bettelheim. Therefore, inverting orthodox ideas, he says: "We are not offended if they classify us among the underdeveloped countries. Because the development of the conscience, our social development and our general culture: these are the prerequisites of our economic and industrial development. In this country, the same as in any other country with similar conditions, people's political and moral development will be needed, *sine qua non*, in order to win the battle against an underdeveloped economy" (Speech of January 12, 1968).

The new Cuban Communist Party and Mella's legacy

While North American imperialism tries to sow disunity, mutual distrust and division ("divide and conquer"), from the beginning Fidel Castro relies on unity between the different factions within the Cuban revolution. The first organization of the different groups is created in July of 1961 under the name of Integrated Revolutionary Organizations (ORI); later, on March 26, 1962, the group is renamed as the Union Party of the Cuban Socialist Revolution, until finally, on October 3, 1965, they assume the unique name that represents them all. They become known as the Cuban Communist Party.

Six years after taking power, the different revolutionary organizations have chosen a name that represents our shared dreams: our unified party will be called Communist.

By choosing the label of "communist"—somewhat after the Young Communist's Union adopts this name in 1962—Fidel Castro reclaims the forgotten heritage of Julio Antonio Mella and the heroic Communist Party of the 1920s. This first Cuban party, prior to Stalinism and the compromises with Batista, continues to be highly respected for its denial of imperialism and its radicalism in its resistance to the Machado dictatorship. Later, the rebel youth before the revolution used the name "communist" as well. The new Cuban Communist Party built by Fidel tries to follow these examples.

Che: Fidel's international delegate

During the first years of the revolution, Fidel Castro sends Che Guevara on several trips to Africa and Asia to arrange alliances between Cuba and anti-imperialist revolutions throughout the world. Guevara visits many countries. His first trip begins on October 10, 1960. He visits Madrid, Prague, Moscow (where he pays homage to Lenin), Beijing (where he meets with Mao), Korea, Moscow again, East Germany, and then Prague again. At Fidel's request, he establishes numerous trade agreements with the Eastern Bloc countries.

Fidel told me to offer them our help.
We fight for world revolution.
The people of Africa, Asia, and
Latin America are
our brothers.

Much later, on another international visit in which Che acts as Fidel's official Cuban envoy, he meets with African and Asian leaders. He operates according to an unequivocal command: help all anti-colonial rebels, and arrange Cuban collaboration with Africa, from the Congo to Angola. The trip begins in the US (where on December 11, 1964, Guevara represents Cuba at the United Nations) and continues to Algeria, Mali, Brazzaville (where he meets with Agostinho Neto of the MPLA), Guinea, Ghana, Dahomey, Algeria, China, Tanzania (where he meets with armed African leaders, including those from the Congo), the United Arab Emirates, back to Algeria, and then to Cairo. All of Che's offers, including to the National Council of the Congolese Revolution, are not based on Che's own initiative, but rather according to Fidel's plans.

Fidel assassinated Che?

Following Fidel's plans for Africa, on April 2, 1965, Guevara leaves Havana to join 120 black Cuban military instructors in the struggle for Congo-Leopoldville against the white Belgian racists. Fidel sends, along with Che, the Communist Party's organizational secretary and other top-rate volunteer combat squads. When Che does not appear in public, the CIA takes advantage of the situation by spreading rumors, trying to sow seeds of intrigue and division between the two revolutionaries, and disseminates through the media—as always—a false story: "*Castro assassinated Che!!*", according to a supposedly "informative" wire from the United Press International on February 6, 1965.

Cuban involvement does not succeed in defeating the Belgian colonists in Africa, who enjoy money, better weapons, and European mercenaries. Che and the Cubans are forced to leave the Congo. Later, considering Che's frustration in Congo-Leopoldville, Fidel sends soldiers and doctors to support the independence of the Congo-Brazzaville, as well as the liberation of Angola and Guinea-Bissau.

Breaking news!
Guevara disappears!
Assassinated by the
dictator, Castro!

I don't understand why
Fidel, who is white,
helps us so much. And
I don't understand why
Che, who is also white,
is ready to die for our
liberty.

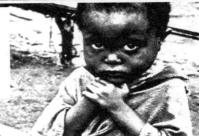

Was there a fight between Fidel and Che?

While leading the Cuban fighters in the Congo, Che Guevara sends a letter which Fidel reads to the newborn Cuban Communist Party on October 3, 1965:

"Year of Agriculture"
Havana
Fidel;
...I feel I have completed the part of my duty that attached me to the Cuban revolution in its territory, and I say goodbye to you, to our comrades, to your people that have become mine. ...Taking account of my life, I believe I have worked with the honor and dedication that was needed to strengthen the revolution. My one serious failure is not to have confided in you more from the first moments in the Sierra Maestra, and not to have understood quickly enough your qualities as a leader and a revolutionary. I have lived through magnificent days, and felt at your side the pride of belonging to our people in the most luminous and sad days of the Carribean crisis. Few times has a statesman shone so brilliantly as in those days. I am proud of myself also for having followed you without wavering, having identified with your manner of thinking and seeing and appreciating both the dangers and the principles of it.

Other lands of the world will now claim my modest efforts... to new battlefields I will carry the faith inculcated within me, the revolutionary spirit of my people, the sensation of complying with the most sacred of duties: to fight against imperialism wherever it is; this comforts and fully heals all wounds...If my final hour arrives beneath different skies, my last thought will be of the Cuban people and especially of you. How I thank you for your lessons and your example, to which I will try to be faithful in every detail of my actions. I have always been identified with the foreign policies of our revolution, and this will continue to be true. Wherever I end up, I will feel the responsibility of being a Cuban revolutionary, and as such I will act.

Until eternal victory, Homeland or Death! I embrace you with all my revolutionary fervor,
Che

The Tricontinental Conference

In January 1966, Cuba convenes the first Conference of Solidarity of the People of Asia, Africa, and Latin America. Delegates and representatives from eighty-two groups meet in Havana, including nations—Vietnam, the USSR, and China—as well as social and political movements. They form three political blocs: the USSR and its allies, China and its followers, and the third, made up of Cuba, Vietnam, and the majority of the revolutions in the Third World.

Internationalism is the key to all revolutions. The politics of "great power" and the rivalries between socialist brothers can't compare with our spirit of struggle, rebellion, and solidarity.

At the closing of the conference, Fidel expounds on the Cuban strategy for world revolution: "In many other parts of America, all of the conditions for revolutionary armed struggle exist ... The combination of imperialist forces on this continent, the proximity of imperialism's metropolitan areas, the jealousy with which imperialism will try to defend its areas of influence in this part of the world—all of this calls for a common strategy, a common and simultaneous struggle ... Sooner or later, all people, or nearly all people, will have to take up arms to free themselves. We believe that in this continent—and among all, or nearly all, of the people on it—this struggle will take on a violent form" (Speech of January 17, 1966).

Fidel in the Tricontinental

Reclaiming the forgotten heritage of Lenin (the founder of the Communist International, later dissolved by Stalin in 1943), as well as the liberated continental perspective of San Martín, Bolívar, and Martí, Fidel closes the Tricontinental Conference by affirming: "Our weapons are defensive, but our men, with all their hearts, are militant revolutionary fighters, ready to struggle against the imperialists anywhere in the world ... The world is large and the imperialists are everywhere. For the Cuban revolutionaries, the field of battle against imperialism embraces the entire world!" (Speech of January 17, 1966).

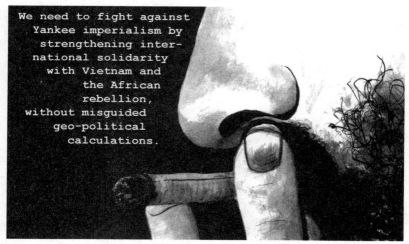

We need to fight against Yankee imperialism by strengthening international solidarity with Vietnam and the African rebellion, without misguided geo-political calculations.

In the Tricontinental Conference, the delegates from Vietnam, Angola, Cape Verde, Mozambique, Laos, and Cambodia, together with Cuba, occupy a fundamental place. To them and to other fighting people in the Third World, Fidel explains: "When Cuba defied imperialist threats, it was not a country that possessed millions of men and an excess of weapons, nor was it a country that possessed thermonuclear weapons. Here, our firepower comes from morals, and the number of men is not infinite, but the dignity and the decorum of this people are ... Imperialism will be defeated. Who has taught us this extraordinary lesson? The people of Vietnam" (Speech of January 17, 1966). In his "Message to the Peoples of the World from the Tricontinental," Che Guevara—away from Cuba during the conference—sent a message in agreement with Fidel, and put forward the slogan: "We must create two, three, many Vietnams."

Che's return to Cuba and meeting with Fidel

Before the defeat in the Congo, Fidel entreats Che to return to Cuba. In a letter (unpublished, but made public in 1999), Fidel suggests to Che that he return and wait for a while before he joins other struggles, with the idea of returning to fight "in the land of Carlitos" (an allusion to Carlos Gardel, meaning Argentina):"Wasn't it the case that Marx, Engels, Lenin, Bolívar, and Martí had to suffer periods of waiting, waiting that sometimes lasted for decades? For you, I don't intend a wait that lasts decades, or even years, but only a few months" (unpublished letter from Fidel to Che, June 1966). Taking his advice, Guevara secretly returns to Cuba to prepare for the revolutionary struggle in Bolivia—the second attempt at an insurgency in the south; the first had been his friend Masetti's, with the EGP.

Che transforms his face, shaving his beard and wearing glasses, in order to pass through international airports without being recognized by the CIA. He meets several times with Fidel and asks Fidel's opinion of his disguise. There are photographs of these final meetings between the two friends, supposedly "enemies," according to the CIA's version.

Fidel and OLAS

In the Tricontinental Conference of 1966, the pro-Soviet group, the pro-China group, and the Vietnamese-Cuban group are all present. In 1967, Cuba convenes the first Conference of the Latin American Organization for Solidarity (OLAS). Strategy is Fidel's primary concern. When closing the OLAS, he affirms: "There is a theory, forty years old now; the famous theory concerning the role of the native bourgeoisie. How much paper, how many high expressions, how much hot air has been used up while waiting for the arrival of a middle class that is liberal, progressive, anti-imperialist ... The essence of the question is whether they can make the masses believe that a revolutionary movement—that socialism—will take power without a struggle, peacefully. And that is a lie!" (Speech of August 10, 1967).

We are Marxist-Leninists.

The revolution is continental, against imperialism and the "native bourgeoisie"

Armed struggle is the road to socialism.

The duty of every revolutionary is to create the revolution.

In the final statement, there are twenty conclusions in defense of "armed struggle and revolutionary violence, the highest expression of the people's fight, the most concrete possibility for defeating imperialism." The conclusion holds that: "The so-called 'national' bourgeoisie of Latin America has an organizational fault: it is interwoven with the master landowners, with whom it forms an oligarchy, as well as the professional armies; it is incapable, absolutely impotent, when it comes to facing imperialism and liberating our countries ... Armed insurrection is the true way of the second war of independence" (General Declaration of OLAS, August 1967).

Fidel and the legacy of San Martín and Bolívar

In the wars for American independence, from 1810 forward, San Martín in the south and Bolívar in the north develop a continental strategy. The Latin Americans triumph against colonialism and achieve their first political independence. But the newborn republics—dominated by oligarchs and the native bourgeoisie—continue social oppression internally and economic dependence externally. A century and a half later, the second continental struggle for independence is born, set against all oppression and dependence. From 1960 on, there is a renewed focus on continental strategy, headed, after the Cuban revolution, by Fidel and Che.

In all of the Latin American revolutionary organizations that, since the 1960s, have been inspired by the thinking of Fidel and Che, references appear to the wars for independence of 1810. For example, in Argentina, the PRT-ERP takes as its own the flag used by San Martín's Army of the Andes (which represents the first war for independence), to which they add a red star (representing socialism and the second war for independence).

Fidel and religion

Among the revolutionaries of OLAS, followers of Marx, Lenin, Fidel, and Che, there are Christians. But in Cuba, the Catholic Church rejects the revolution. At the same time, the revolution's leaders (with the exception of the Christian J. A. Echeverría) are generally against the priesthood. During the first years of the revolution, this leads to mutual misunderstanding (one expression of this being the "Military Units to Aid Production," prison camps in which some Christians were unjustly punished). Nevertheless, after the formation of OLAS, Cuba is open to Christian revolutionaries, influenced by the radicalization of the theology of liberation. (An excellent book: *Fidel and Religion*, an interview with the Brazilian theologian Friar Betto, 1985.) Today, the example of Camilo Torres Restrepo, a priest who died in combat, an admirer of Fidel, and a Colombian guerilla, is held up as an example by many believing Christians both inside and outside Cuba.

Camilo Torres

The duty of every Christian is to fight against the false gods of money and the worshipers of the golden calf.

Fidel

Revolutionaries, Marxists and other believers, we all want to create a world where a person is worth much more than all the gold in the world.

May Shangó, Eleguá, and Ogún protect you so the gringos don't take over our country.

In contrast to Christianity and its complicated status within the revolution, there is Santería, the religion of former African slaves. Not answering to any outside authority, such as the reactionary Vatican, Santería allows for a great degree of synchronicity with the socialist ideology that the revolution adopts early on. The revolution and Santería coexist from the beginning, although only in recent years has Santería received any degree of social recognition.

Homosexuality in Cuba

Although there is a very strong prejudice against homosexuals in the 1930s in Cuba—a part of the cultural heritage of Spanish tradition and Catholicism that goes back for centuries, far older than the Cuban revolution—and although there is unjust discrimination against them, no small number of the major intellectuals and writers of the Cuban revolution are homosexuals. In the twenty-first century, this prejudice is slowly fading, and the Cuban government itself leads a public campaign against discrimination.

> To be gay or to be a revolutionary? And who said that gays can't be anti-imperialist and anti-capitalist?

Today in Cuba, homosexuality and various other ways of showing sexual diversity are promoted, encouraged, and publicly debated. For example, there is a special foundation, funded and supported by the state and well known to the public (headed by Mariela Castro, Fidel's niece and Raúl's daughter), that puts on events and activities, sponsors debates, publishes magazines, and heads a political campaign against old traditionalist prejudices. Their journals are available, in addition to information about the Center and its activities, on their website at www.cenesex.sld.cu. There is also a beautiful Cuban film, *Fresa y Chocolate* (*Strawberries and Chocolate*, 1993), directed by Tomás Gutiérrez Alea and produced by the Cuban Institute of the Arts and Cinematographic Industry (ICAIC), in which homosexuality is defended and the homophobic prejudices of pseudo-revolutionaries are disputed.

Bolivia and Che's continental strategy

Trying to bring Fidel and the Cuban revolution's continental and world strategy into practice, Che Guevara plans to continue the revolution in the south of Latin America. He tries to "create two, three, many Vietnams" so that imperialism will have to divide its forces. His plan is to open a new battle front (and provide insurrectional training) in Bolivia, through which groups of insurgents will be able to travel to the many nations of the South: Peru, Brazil, and, above all, Argentina, Che's homeland.

Peasant: We have already been working with Che and Piñeiro in helping Masetti. Many miners supported Guevara: they were massacred. The "official history" conceals this, so as to ridicule Che.
Che: Those who criticize me for choosing Bolivia ignore the heroic struggle and rebellion of the Bolivian people, who defeated the army in 1952.

To carry out this strategy, Fidel finally accepts Che's proposal to return to Cuba—after his frustrated experience in the Congo and his secret journey through Tanzania and Czechoslovakia. In Cuba, Che trains and changes his appearance. Previously, Guevara had sent a covert agent to Bolivia to gather information: the Argentinean Haydée Tamara Bunke Bíder (alias Tania, although in Bolivia she uses the name Laura Martínez Bauer), who infiltrates the highest levels of the military dictatorship, where the CIA has supported the head Bolivian military men, such as General Barrientos. Tania died fighting together with other guerrillas on August 31, 1967.

Fidel's support for Che

While training in Cuba, Guevara chooses his fighters for the south of Latin America. Among them are members of the central committee of the Cuban Communist Party, who accompany him to Bolivia with the full support of Fidel, Raúl Castro, and Barbarroja, who is in charge of coordinating secret insurgent operations in Latin America. Among the Cuban survivors of Bolivia are Antonio Villegas Tamayo, alias "Pombo," who had accompanied Che in the Sierra Maestra, the Congo, and Bolivia, and who, after Guevara's death, goes to fight in Angola. Fidel gives him the medal of a "Hero of the Republic of Cuba." In 2006, Pombo is the general of the Revolutionary Armed Forces of Cuba.

profound suffering

Che did not go to Bolivia alone! Some of the best Fidel had accompanied him. The majority died fighting together with Che.

The Bolivian army, a group of commandos, and CIA operative Félix Rodríguez capture Che on October 7, 1967, then murder him on October 9. Rodríguez, who plays a major part in this cold-blooded murder, is an anti-Castroist from Miami who participates in the repression of El Salvador, the counterrevolution in Nicaragua, and in Operation Condor with Pinochet and Videla.

Fidel in the face of Che's assassination

After Che's death, Fidel says: "Che and those who died in his international army are heroes. They are mistaken, those who sing of victory and believe that his physical death means the death of his ideas and his example. Every day that passes, he grows more gigantic in the hearts of the people, because he carried the ideas of Marxism and Leninism to their most pure expression, their most fresh and revolutionary. If they ask us how we want to be, our people, our military, our fighters, our sons and our future generations ... We want to be like Che!" (Speech of October 18, 1967).

Those who slandered me in 1965 for assassinating Che later accused me of having him killed in Bolivia.

It's known that the slander comes from the same CIA who ordered the assassination of our comrades.

Referring to Mario Monge and the other pro-Soviets who betray Che, Fidel affirms: "The pseudo-revolutionaries, opportunists, and charlatans who, conceiving of themselves as Marxists, communists, and other things, have not wavered in classifying Che as mistaken, an adventurer, an idealist, who think his death is the swan song of the revolutionary struggle in Latin America ... How many of these miserable people will find joy in the death of Che! They justify it to themselves, or to treasonous leaders who never hesitate to put the brakes on revolutionary action, because they do not want to fight, nor will they ever want to fight, for the people and their freedom. They have caricatured revolutionary ideas and changed the organizations of revolutionary struggle into the tools of conciliation with the exploiters, both internal and external" ("A Necessary Introduction to the *Diary of Che in Bolivia*," 1967). In spite of this betrayal, young communists like Loyola Guzmán, Inti, and Coco Peredo fight to the end together with Guevara.

Cuban revolutionary thought

Along with the political offensive of the Tricontinental Conference and OLAS, Cuba also promotes an ideological battle against "reformism" in social thinking. ("Reformism" consists of proposing palliatives, bandages, and other makeshift repairs to capitalism in order to make the system less brutal, but without fundamentally changing it.) If *Casa de las Américas* and the first era of *El Caimán Barbudo* were the major literary and cultural magazines, the most important social science magazine that the Cuban revolution produces is *Pensamiento Crítico*. Fifty-three issues are published between 1967 and 1971, each nearly two hundred pages long.

The dogmatists accuse us of "heresy." One must empower oneself to act with one's own mind.

Just after the Tricontinental and the OLAS, Fidel convenes the Cultural Congress of Havana. Before intellectuals of seventy countries, he affirms: "At times, we have seen supposed members of the vanguard in the deepest part of the rear guard in the fight against imperialism! While many supposed members of the vanguard remain silent and motivate no one, we have seen many working-class intellectuals motivate themselves and raise their voice against imperialism in Vietnam, against the murder of our comrade Che Guevara in Bolivia, in defense of the black movement in the US. Because of this, we value most highly the work of the working-class intellectuals, those of the Third World, but also those of Europe and the United States! Marxism must develop as a revolutionary force, not as a pseudo-revolutionary church!" (Speech of January 12, 1968).

Fidel and European intellectuals

In contrast to the Eastern Bloc (the USSR and its allies) who disparage Western intellectualism, Fidel establishes from the beginning of the revolution a circle of alliances with the intellectual workers of Europe—writers, thinkers, editors, and artists. The Frenchman François Maspero (b. 1932) and the Italian Giangiacomo Feltrinelli (1926–72), both editors, spread the thinking of the Cuban revolution in their respective languages.

> Thank you for your support, dear friends! We are quite sure. Culture is fundamental in the battle of ideas! To depreciate the intellectuals "in the name of Marxism" is a scandalously stupid thing.

Simone de Beauvoir, Jean-Paul Sartre and Fidel

At the beginning of the 1960s, Jean-Paul Sartre (1905–86) and Simone de Beauvoir (1908–86) visit the island and publish articles about the Cuban revolution in their magazine, *Les Temps Modernes*. According to later evidence from former CIA agents, North American intelligence closely follows Sartre's magazine, trying to counteract European cultural support for Cuba. Fidel continues the same discourse today in magazines like *Le Monde diplomatique* and others of the same style.

Fidel and the student movement

Fidel's first political skills are developed at the end of the 1940s on the hill of the University of Havana. Almost twenty years later, when he is already the leader of the revolution, Fidel returns to the Plaza de Cadenas at the University and there attends many assemblies and discussions with Cuban students.

The Cuban revolution and its ideology—from Fidel Castro and Che Guevara to Minister of Education Armando Hart Dávalos, everyone who began in the University struggle—constitute, on an international level, the link between the two great student rebellions of 1918 and 1968. The first rebellions come from South America (born in Cordoba, Argentina, and spreading through Mexico and Cuba); the second are made in Europe and North America (from the most radical in Germany to the most famous in France, during May of 1968, and continuing through the United States). Cuba connects both cultural universes. Fidel is a child of the University Reform in Cordoba—from which he takes ideas from Mella, Roa, and the turn-of-the-century generation—and in turn he influences Europe in 1968.

In this university I made myself a revolutionary. Our slogan is: "study, work, and the rifle." Youth should be the vanguard!

The Cuban revolution's influence in the US

The influence of Fidel, Che, and the Cuban revolution does not stop with European intellectuals and students. It also penetrates the culture of the US. Fidel Castro does not appeal only to the radical militancy of the Black Panthers, or to Malcolm X. He also gains the enthusiastic support of famous intellectuals like the three editors of the celebrated *Monthly Review*, Paul Baran (1910–64), Paul M. Sweezy (1910–2004), and Leo Huberman (1903–68), as well as Charles Wright Mills (1916–62) and Herbert Marcuse (1898–1979), who defends Guevara's ideas when he travels to Germany in 1967.

The majority of the North American intellectuals that visit Cuba to meet with Fidel write books defending the revolution. Charles Wright Mills in 1960 publishes the famous *Listen Yanqui! (The Revolution in Cuba)*, and Leo Huberman and Paul Sweezy co-write *Cuba: Anatomy of a Revolution*; in 1961 Paul Baran writes *Reflections on the Cuban Revolution* and Waldo Frank (1889–1967) writes *The Prophetic Island: A Portrait of Cuba*, and in 1967 Maurice Zeitlin, after traveling throughout the island, writes his doctoral thesis at Princeton, entitled *Revolutionary Politics and the Cuban Working Class*. The same happens with several film directors, the latest being Oliver Stone, who in 2002 films *Comandante*, a long interview with Fidel.

The Cuban revolution and Latin American culture

From 1959 forward, Cuba becomes a beacon for the entire critical culture of the continent. For the first time, Latin American works are translated in reverse: from Spanish to English, French, Italian, etc., inverting the traditional way in which culture spreads from the center of an empire to its provinces. Cuba's cultural influence spreads throughout Latin America. Starting with the "boom" of the new Latin American novel in the 1960s—led by Alejo Carpentier with magical realist works like *El reino de este mundo* (*The Kingdom of this World*, 1949)—and continuing with the spread of the theory of dependence and the radicalization of liberation theology, as well as several vanguard aesthetics (such as the "Vietnam" and "Tucumán Arde" expositions in 1966 and 1968 in Argentina).

The history of our America, of her culture and her revolutions, is nothing more than a chronicle of magical realism.

ALEJO CARPENTIER.

The same happens with the systemization of popular education and the *Pedagogy of the Oppressed*, and with the new Latin American cinema. In all areas, in all trends of thought, and in all points of view, one can hear the echoes of the earthquake that the Cuban revolution causes across the continent in traditional thinking and in the methods of cultural production, exchange, reception, and consumption.

The rise and fall of the Latin American insurgency

Starting with the continental impulse that Fidel and Che give to the revolution, throughout Latin America revolutionary organizations spring up to fight against military dictatorships and imperialism and to try to achieve national liberation, democracy, and socialism. A new generation of young militants—workers from both the city and the country, students, intellectuals, and even committed priests—make the rebel flag of the Cuban revolution their own. On a continental scale, there is a resurgence of the fighting political and ideological spirit of the Latin American Marxism of the 1920s.

The most reactionary circles of the elite who govern the US do not remain passive when confronted with this wave of Latin American rebellion. Financiers, the military, intelligence agents, and the strategists of imperialism: all are alike in working actively to repress the insurgency and to maintain their social domination by means of a brutal and bloody genocide.

The war of counterinsurgency

To put an end to the insurgency, Yankee armed forces train thousands and thousands of Latin American military and police in performing coups d'état, kidnappings, torture, and the massive "disappearances" of dissidents. "We must end the example of Cuba with blood and fire!" is their slogan. Thus they sum up the theory of national security and counterinsurgent or counterrevolutionary wars that the Yankees and their Latin American students import from France and the ultra-right extremists in Algeria.

Henry Kissinger

We're the guarante of peace, tranquility, individual liberty and the "open society" in the West. We've succeeded in isolating Cuba in Latin America!

The first wave of Latin American insurgency that was born with the Cuban revolution is defeated; its major revolutionary groups are wiped out; its militants, in the best Nazi style, are exterminated. Cuba ends the crucial and emblematic decade of the 1960s by being completely isolated in the face of the aggressive military power of the United States.

Cuba's growing isolation

At the end of the 1960s, the US tightens its grip on the western hemisphere, strangling all social rebellions with coups d'état, interventions by the CIA, and multiple massacres that drown Latin American insurgencies and their bases of support in blood. Meanwhile, on the other side of the world, the Soviet Union—in a complete break with China—invades Czechoslovakia.

They killed our comrades in Latin America. We are alone. One isolated revolution can not survive for long. But we will not surrender! We will not give ourselves up!
                                    —Fidel

From the high point of the Tricontinental Conference and the OLAS to the death of Che Guevara in Bolivia and the crushing of other Latin American revolutions, little by little Cuba finds itself alone in its confrontation with the savage giant to the north.

Economic problems and joining CAME

With no end to the US blockade, on March 13, 1968, the Cuban economic leadership launches an all-out frontal offensive: a massive state takeover, including the nationalization of small businesses, creating totally free telephone and water services, a war on bureaucracy, and the virtual "disappearance" of money from exchanges between socialist businesses—transactions are now made without the intervention of markets. Although at first glance this seems like an application of Guevara's ideas, in reality this is a different model, since the nationalization is not accompanied by strict accountability, causing disorganization and the squandering of resources. This is the state of things when the economic leadership plans to produce ten million tons of sugar in 1970. They do not meet their goal (producing only 8.5 million.) The fiasco of the "harvest of the ten million" results in major changes to economic policy.

Welcome to CAME!
You will receive Soviet help,
but forget about
industrialization...
we'll worry about that
ourselves,
heh, heh, heh...
You give us the primary
materials... nickel
and sugar.

The continued Yankee blockade, the weakness of the economy (where there exist, at the same time, two antagonistic systems: the budgetary system of financing, centered on city planning, and economic calculation, centered on the market), the delays in industrialization, and the "harvest of the ten million" fiasco: all of these oblige Cuba in 1972 to enter into the Council for Mutual Economic Assistance (CAME). Thirteen years after the triumph of the revolution, the revolutionary leadership must postpone the dream of industrial autonomy. The USSR and its associates are against the Cuban industrialization recommended by Che. Instead, they suggest a "socialist division of labor" (in which Cuba exports raw materials in exchange for Soviet technology).

The "Padilla Affair" and the "Quinquenio gris"

Isolated yet politically tied to the USSR, Cuba is hit by the "Padilla Affair."

Between 1956 and 1959, the Cuban writer Heberto Padilla (1932–2000) works peacefully in Miami, ignorant of the revolution. In 1959, he returns to Cuba. Between 1962 and 1964, he works freelance jobs, among them as a news correspondent in London, Prague, and Moscow. He works with the magazine *Unión*. In 1968, Padilla wins the Cuban Writers and Artists Union (UNEAC) award for his book *Fuera de Juego (Out of the Game)*, which, although controversial, is published in Cuba. He works for the university from 1968 to 1971. This same year, he reads his book *Provocaciones* at the UNEAC. On March 20, 1971, he is placed under house arrest. He offers a sham "self-criticism," parodying the show trials in Moscow in 1936. He continues to work for the university and as a translator. He is freed in 1980, and goes to the US. Padilla's imprisonment damages the international reputation of the revolution among many European intellectuals (Sartre, Simone de Beauvoir, and Susan Sontag protest, among others).

Although the "Padilla Affair" is used by the enemies of the revolution to compare Cuba with the USSR under Stalin, Padilla's imprisonment is an unfortunate decision, encouraged by the sectarian and bureaucratic core of the National Council of Culture. In the climate of distress and isolation, those currents of Cuban thought that are closest to the USSR become dominant. During this period, the journal *Pensamiento Crítico* closes, as does the philosophy department of the University of Havana—totally apart from the Padilla Affair—the department which generated the most original thinking from the Cuban revolution. So begins, in culture and in the social sciences, the "gray five years" (*Quinquenio Gris*, coined by the Cuban writer Ambrosio Fornet). In this new climate, the cultural institutions that maintain the creativity of the earlier period are *Casa de las Américas*, the ICAIC, and the Cuban National Ballet.

I criticize the decision, but I won't become part of the campaign against the revolution. The enemies of Cuba would use this error to attack socialism and Fidel.

Julio Cortázar.

157

University education for the masses and internationalism

Owing to Cuba's total isolation from the rest of Latin America at the beginning of the 1970s, Soviet ideology gains strength. The use of Soviet textbooks in the education system increases, and Soviet ideology will dominate education until 1986. Nevertheless, this new pedagogic orientation—very different from in the 1960s—arrives along with an increased access to universities. These were previously restricted to an "illustrious minority," as in capitalism, and now they become a real and concrete possibility for the majority of the population. Illiteracy becomes nothing but a sad memory of the prerevolutionary past.

We remain isolated in Latin America due to the failure of our friends' revolutions ... we had to enter into CAME with the Soviets. But we will not surrender! We will continue fighting! Now in Africa, against the racist regimes and colonialists.

Nelson Mandela & Fidel.

Notwithstanding its closer relationship with the USSR, the Cuban revolution manages to maintain its vitality. In the 1970s, Fidel continues to insist on militant internationalism, now much more important than in the previous period, as an antidote to any temptation to extinguish or moderate the anti-imperialist urge, to bureaucratize the socialist revolution, or to freeze the process of social transformation. This political decision by Fidel—centered primarily on providing help and solidarity to anti-colonial struggles in Africa, although also in Latin America—is aimed at keeping alive the spirit of rebellion and anti-dogmatism that has characterized the Cuban revolution since its birth.

Salvador Allende and the "peaceful way to socialism"

In 1970, the doctor Salvador Allende wins the elections in Chile and becomes the head of the government, along with the People's Unity Party (UP), the party of the left. The UP is made up of socialists, communists, radicals, and Christians of the left. Allende belongs to the most moderate part of the UP, although he is a close friend of Cuba and Fidel. When Che dies in Bolivia, three Cuban survivors manage to escape and make their way to Chile. They are detained in Iquique. Allende intercedes in order to have them transferred to Santiago, and goes with them to Tahiti to deliver them to the Cuban ambassador there. Later, when he is president, he travels to Cuba, and on December 13, 1972, he speaks in the Plaza of the Revolution, together with Fidel. There, he swears on his life to defend socialism. Allende's political strategy—popularly known as the "Chilean way to socialism"—consists of slowly and patiently moving toward socialism through legal, parliamentary, and institutional means, without armed struggle, arming the population, or civil war. This thinking coincides, on the international level, with the strategy the USSR has advocated since the time of Khrushchev, known as the "peaceful transition to socialism" (officially sanctioned by all of the Communist Parties in the world, including the Chilean party, at the International Conference of the Communist Party of 1960).

Fidel with Salvador Allende. Behind them, Pinochet.

Fidel, Allende, and Miguel Enríquez

Invited by Salvador Allende, Fidel Castro visits Chile from November 10 to December 4, 1971. During this long stay, Fidel meets with miners, students, and peasants. Even the future dictator and murderer Augusto Pinochet—a supposed military "constitutionalist"—must greet the Cuban leader with honors. Fidel bids farewell to the people in the National Stadium of Santiago de Chile on December 2, 1971.

The fascists, urged on and trained by the CIA, are preparing for a coup-d'état. You need to unite yourselves and be alert!

Comrade Allende: to head the government is not the same as coming to power! To oppose the coming coup, you must fortify the people's power and arm the public.

Miguel Enríquez

In all of his trips and meetings, Fidel—repudiated by the local ultra-right—tries to unite the Chilean left. Despite this, a real strategic division exists at the core of the Chilean revolutionaries between the "peaceful way" (the moderates of the Socialist and Communist Parties) and those who recommend the creation of a military force of the people (the Left of the Socialist Party). These last are headed by the Revolutionary Left Movement (MIR), whose leader is the young Miguel Enríquez (1944–74), a personal friend of Fidel. The MIR, despite not belonging to the People's Unity Party, warns the UP against a possible coup d'état, and supports arming groups of industrial workers to support Allende.

Fidel's aid to Allende

In Chile, Fidel supports the nationalization of the copper mines and other businesses. Cuba donates a million dollars for printing books on a massive scale. Fidel gives Allende as a personal gift an AK-47 automatic rifle (which Allende uses on the day of the coup), advising him about the dangerousness of the Chilean bourgeoisie. Later, from Havana, Fidel writes to him: "I see that now that the issue is the dialogue between the Party and the truck owners' strike. I can imagine the tension, and your desire to gain some time, to improve the organization of your forces in case fighting breaks out ... If the other side is set on perfidious, irresponsible politics, don't forget for a second the strength of the Chilean working class, and the energetic support that it has offered you in all of your difficult moments; it can, at your request, or when the revolution is in danger, paralyze those who would carry out a coup d'état, maintain the fortitude of those who would waver, set its own terms for living, and decide, for once, if it's the right time, the destiny of Chile" (Letter from Fidel to Allende, July 29, 1973).

Learning much later of Allende's death, Fidel notes: "Salvador Allende showed more dignity, more honor, more valor, and more heroism than all the fascist military put together. The fascists have told the world about the rifle with which Allende fought, the automatic rifle that we gave him, trying to create coarse, ridiculous propaganda with it. But the facts have shown that no gift could have been better for President Allende than that automatic rifle for defending the government of the People's Unity Party! Much reasoning and premonition went into our giving that rifle to the president. And if every worker and every peasant had held a rifle like that in his hands, there would have been no fascist coup! That is the great lesson that falls to the revolutionaries from out of the events in Chile" (Speech of September 28, 1973).

> If he had distributed arms among the workers of Chile...
>
> ... history would be different!

Pinochet, the US, and the birth of neoliberalism

On September 11, 1973, besieged at the presidential palace by artillery fire, tanks, and aerial bombers, Allende keeps his word. He resists heroically, his head protected by a helmet, the rifle in his hand (he even fires a bazooka at a fascist tank), until there is no way out. He retreats to his family and his staff and he shoots himself. He will not give the fascists the pleasure of seeing him surrender. His daughter Beatriz remembers how, thinking of Miguel Enríquez, Allende vows: "I will not move from here [the Moneda Palace], I will fulfill, until my death, the responsibilities of President that the people have entrusted to me. Now it is your turn, Miguel…" Allende had ordered the Cuban embassy—surrounded on September 11, 1973, by the military—to bring weapons to the MIR on the day of the coup.

Down with Cuba!
Long live the market!
America for the North Americans!

Today it is public knowledge (per the US State Department's Hinchey Report) that Pinochet's coup was financed in part by the telecommunications giant International Telephone and Telegraph (ITT). According to Stella Calloni's book *Operation Condor: Criminal Pact* (Havana: Ciencias Sociales, 2005), an analysis of CIA documents (declassified on November 14, 2000) proves that the CIA and ITT carried out many secret operations intended to depose Allende and to assist Pinochet's coup. The fascist military leaders and the terrorist groups from the extreme right who bring down Allende's government, like "Patria y Libertad" (Homeland and Freedom), are trained by North American intelligence. Many of these groups later participate in Operation Condor and in counterinsurgency operations on the continent. The film *Missing*, starring Jack Lemmon and directed by Costa Gavras, illustrates the role the CIA takes in Chile. With Pinochet, the first experiments in neoliberalism on a world level are born—in blood, torture, and death—the predecessors of Margaret Thatcher's actions in England and Ronald Reagan's in the US.

"National security" and Operation Condor

Although there are coups d'état before Chile, such as the one in Brazil in 1964 or in Argentina in 1966, the fierce military dictatorship of Pinochet inaugurates a new era in the 1970s. With these methods, the US tries to reclaim, on its "back porch," the initiative that it had begun to lose in Asia and Africa. Through Pinochet and the CIA, the US creates the doctrine of "national security," which carries out systematic torture and wars of counterinsurgency across the entire continent. William Colby, director of the CIA, is the inspiration behind the Phoenix Program—the torture and murder of more than twenty thousand Viet Cong guerillas. US military instructors apply the same methods across Latin America.

In the organization of the counterrevolutionary war in Latin America, Operation Condor—the coordination among different military dictatorships of efforts to repress revolutionary groups—is fundamental. The anti-Castro extremists of Miami play a distinguished role in Operation Condor, under orders from the CIA, and headed by Orlando Bosch, Luis Posada Carriles, Hernán Ricardo, and Freddy Lugo, among other full-time terror professionals. Part of this group bases itself in Pinochet's Chile, from which it operates throughout southern Latin America.

Pinochet

Videla

Stroessner

Banzer

These are my pigeons. They're cheap, and they do all the dirty work: kidnapping and assassination, all so we can impose capitalism and increase profits.

The victory of Vietnam

During the Vietnam War, Fidel Castro is the first and only head of state in the world to visit the liberated zones of South Vietnam. There, surrounded by Vietnamese soldiers, he raises the banner of the National Liberation Front. In 1974, President Osvaldo Dorticós and Raúl Castro, commander of the Revolutionary Armed Forces, visit Hanoi, in North Vietnam, where they reiterate their support for the liberation of the South and the reunification of the country.

In April 1975, the National Liberation Front's forces in South Vietnam achieve victory in Saigon (today, Ho Chi Minh City) over the US's puppet regime. There they knock down the bars and enter the North American embassy, supposedly "impregnable." Yankee soldiers who felt very "macho" when bringing down Vietnamese women and children flee, terrified, hanging like cowards from the rudders of the last helicopters. Photos of this will circulate around the world, along with images of Vietnamese people burned alive by napalm. All of the movies Hollywood turns out time and time again about Vietnam can not hide the simple truth: imperialism could be beaten.

Coup in Argentina: the "desaparecidos"

A year after the victory of Vietnam, the Argentinean Armed Forces carry out a new coup d'état on March 26, 1976. A brutal genocide begins. The military dictatorship's intelligence forces know that the major revolutionary organizations receive support from Cuba. To the Argentinean military, Fidel Castro is the devil. Although they kidnap and make thirty thousand people "disappear" on a massive scale, the repression and the terror of Operation Condor are concentrated primarily against the followers of Guevara and Fidel in the southern corner of Latin America. Some of these groups have been working together since 1974, when the Junta for Revolutionary Coordination (JCR) forms between the Argentinean PRT-ERP, the Chilean MIR, the MLN-Tupámaros in Uruguay, and the Bolivian ELN. With the annihilation of these groups, the defeat of the second wave of revolutions in Latin America (after the first wave in the 1960s) is achieved.

After 1976, the team of ultra-right anti-Castro members of the CIA—Orlando Bosch, Luis Posada Carriles, Hernán Ricardo, and Freddy Lugo—take refuge in Pinochet's Chile, and begin to work with General Videla. In Argentina, on August 9, 1976, they torture and "disappear" two members of the Cuban Embassy in Buenos Aires: Jesús Cejas Arias and Crescencio Galareña Hernández.

Support for Africa and the world revolution

Despite his isolation in Latin America, Fidel continues to push for rebellions in the African colonies. The most important of all is Angola, under Portuguese control. On April 25, 1974, the Carnation Revolution succeeds in Portugal—aided by the Marxist general Vasco Gonçalves and the Communist Party, among others. The fall of Portuguese fascism allows the anti-colonial struggle in Africa to grow more intense. Portugal, until that point, ruled the colonies of Angola, Mozambique, Cape Verde, and Guinea-Bissau. After the revolution, the Africans gain their independence.

In Angola there are three political movements, all diametrically opposed: the People's Movement of Angolan Liberation (MPLA), led by Agostinho Neto (1922–79), the National Front of Angolan Liberation (FNLA), led by Holden Roberto (1923–2007), and UNITA, led by Dr. Jonas Zavimbi (1934–2002). While the progressive MPLA has ties with Cuba, the FNLA and UNITA are linked to the racist extreme right of South Africa, led by P. W. Botha, and even have ties with the United States CIA.

Cuba and Angola

Due to its strategic importance, Angola is coveted both from the north by Zaire (led by Sese Seko Mobutu, the murderer of Congolese Prime Minister Patrice Émery Lumumba) and from the south by South Africa (led by the small, white, and racist minority of President P. W. Botha). After the Portuguese retreat, both countries involve themselves in the Angolan Civil War with the help of fierce white mercenaries (financed by the US and by some European countries). Meanwhile, between 1978 and 1986, Fidel sends the "Che Guevara" educational detachment, with two thousand volunteer teachers, to Angola.

The US, France, England, Portugal and Belgium support the white racists. Fidel supports us with weapons, teachers, doctors, and combatants ready to die for our liberty.

In July of 1975, the US President Gerald Ford and his advisor Henry Kissinger attempt a covert operation. They, along with the South African invasion—which begins on August 5, 1975—want to prevent the independence of Angola, planned for November 11, 1975. The offensive becomes widespread in October of 1975. Fidel responds to the MPLA's pleas for help—without consulting the Soviets—and brings help to the victimized people: five hundred Cuban military instructors arrive in October, and on November 5, 1975, he sends a batallion of soldiers with anti-tank weapons: Angolan victory. Fidel explains: "Angola's victory is the twin sister of Playa Girón. Angola, for the Yankee imperialists, is an African Playa Girón" (Speech of April 19, 1976). In June 1976, the blacks of Soweto (in Johannesburg, South Africa) revolt, led by the African National Congress (whose leader Nelson Mandela was cruelly imprisoned from 1964 to 1990). On May 4, 1978, the white South Africans massacre six hundred Namibian refugees in Casigna. In October of 1987, the South African army returns to invade Angola with five thousand soldiers. A conflict arises between the Cubans and the sixty Soviet advisors in Angola about how to respond to this aggression.

The Cuban victory in Angola

To drive out the South Africans, Fidel—as he did in 1975, without consulting the USSR—sends an additional fifty thousand soldiers. Finally, from January to March of 1988, the Cuban forces take command in the last battle at Cuito Cuanavale, where they defeat the UNITA-South African coalition. Cuba, the MPLA in Angola, and the SWAPO from Namibia win the war. Thanks in part to this Cuban victory, the apartheid regime in South Africa comes to an end, and Namibia's independence is recognized (in the first free elections, the SWAPO, the allies of Cuba, are the winners). In December 1988, Cuba, Angola, and South Africa sign a peace agreement in New York. The Cuban fighters return, triumphantly, in January of 1989 with Angola and Namibia independent, and with the black majority of South Africa electing, at last, its first black president: Nelson Mandela from the African National Congress.

The Cuban mission for solidarity with Angola lasts fifteen years. It is known as "Operation Carlota" (Carlota is the name of a black Angolan slave who lived in Cuba in the nineteenth century who rose up against the white masters and died in her rebellion). In total, four hundred fifty thousand Cubans are involved (three hundred eighty thousand soldiers and seventy thousand civilian aides). It is one of the greatest internationalist achievements in world history, along with the International Brigades in Spain and the war of liberation against the Nazis.

If now, thanks to this Castro son-of-a-bitch, the negroes of Africa govern themselves, what will become of our western civilization and Christianity?

Fidel and Mandela against racism and apartheid

The apartheid system in South Africa combines several kinds of social oppression at once, from the neo-Nazi racism of its white minority—defended by the agents of the Bureau of State Security, or BOSS—to the savage exploitation of the South African working class, to its neocolonialist ambitions toward other African countries. The African National Congress, a multiracial project, tries to fight apartheid on all of these grounds. After the Cuban victory over the South African troops, the white minority must accept the end of apartheid.

Listen, Fidel:
How far the slaves and the condemned
people of this world have come!

Explaining the astonishing Cuban aid to Africa, Fidel reflects: "To be an internationalist is to settle our own debts to humanity. Whoever is incapable of fighting for others will never be sufficiently capable of fighting for himself" (Speech of December 5, 1988). In 1977, Isla de la Juventud to the south of Havana receives thousands of Africans on scholarship (who come from the recently-liberated ex-colonies) and other young poor people from the Third World, all of whom travel to Cuba to study for free. They come from Mozambique, Namibia, and Angola, as well as Nicaragua and El Salvador, and many other places besides.

Fidel, the Sandinista Revolution, and Granada

Since Augusto César Sandino (1893–1934) rebelled against the Yankee invasion, Nicaragua has suffered forty-three years of the Somoza family's dictatorship. In 1961, Carlos Fonseca Amador (1936–76), a comrade of Fidel and Che, founds the Sandinista National Liberation Front (FSLN). Fonesca dies fighting in November of 1976. The FSLN then divides into three groups: the proletarian FSLN, the FSLN for the continuation of the people's war, and the insurrectional FSLN. In March of 1979, Fidel tries to reunite them. After the defeat of the insurgency in the 1960s and 1970s, the Sandinista revolution triumphs over Somoza on July 19, 1979. This same year, on March 13, 1979, the revolution on the Caribbean island Granada succeeds, where the New Jewel Movement (MNJ), formed on May 11, 1973, by Maurice Bishop, overthrows a dictatorship of twenty-nine years. The Yankees invade Granada in 1983 and choke the revolution in blood. In addition to Bishop, Fidel is an ally of Michael Manley (1923–97), the prime minster of Jamaica from 1972 to 1980 and 1989 to 1992.

Fidel has been
our teacher.
From the Cuban
revolution,
we learned
to merge Marxism
with our own
traditions.

Carlos Fonseca

During the eleven years of the Sandinista government (1979–90), the Cuban revolution brings thousands of teachers and doctors to Nicaragua. The CIA—with money from the Iran-Contra Affair—organizes groups of counterrevolutionaries who leave fifty thousand people dead. Murdering from their base in Honduras, these groups force the FSLN to establish obligatory military service. This "low-intensity war," imposed by the US, takes its toll on Nicaragua. These circumstances—along with the corruption of some of the FSLN leaders—provoke a crisis for the revolution, which loses in the elections of February 25, 1990.

Fidel and the El Salvador Revolution

With the Sandinista victory in Nicaragua, the revolutionary struggle in El Salvador grows stronger. There, on October 10, 1980, five revolutionary groups, inspired by Cuba's example, come together: the People's Forces of Liberation Farabundo Martí (FPL), the Revolutionary Army of the People (ERP), the National Resistance (RN), the Central American Workers' Revolutionary Party (PRTC), and the Communist Party (PC). Together, they form the Farabundo Martí Front for National Liberation (FMLN). They adopt the name of Augustín Farabundo Martí (1883–1932), the colleague of Sandino in Nicaragua, secretary general of the Communist Party of El Salvador, and the leader of the peasant rebellion of 1932 (in which the oligarchy and its army killed 30,000 of the people of El Salvador).

I have two homelands: Cuba, and my own, El Salvador.

Fidel has taught us the importance of uniting all revolutionary groups.

Roque Dalton

One of the emblematic figures of the El Salvador revolution is the militant and poet Roque Dalton (1935–75), who lives for several years in Cuba. Fidel and the Cuban revolution support the El Salvador revolution and the FMLN. As a countermeasure, during the civil war from 1980 to 1992, the US invests billions of dollars to create the "death squads." One of the terrorists that the CIA sends to fight against the FMLN is Félix Rodríguez, the murderer of Che Guevara in Bolivia. In several videos, this mercenary brags about firing from North American helicopters into the Salvadorian jungle. The FMLN does not succeed in taking power, but neither is it defeated. By 2006, it has become the major political force in El Salvador, with the first president from the FMLN elected on March 15, 2009.

Fidel and the foreign debt crisis

In the 1970s, the price of oil rises. The exporters of oil deposit their massive profits in banks in the US and Europe. These banks, especially the IMF and the World Bank, send the money to dependent countries, primarily to military dictatorships like Argentina, Chile, and Uruguay, who find themselves in debt due to financial fraud. Meanwhile, the "leak of capital" from the Third World continues, and trade imbalances in international commerce grow. In the 1980s, the Yankee banks raise the interest rates on their loans and overvalue the dollar. The debt becomes unpayable!

> The foreign debt of the Third World is not only illegal and immoral, but it's also contracted by military dictatorships and caused by the IMF and the World Bank. In addition, it can't be paid!

Through several meetings in 1985, Fidel calls for an alliance of indebted countries to be created, in order to reestablish an economic order that will cancel the foreign debt of the Third World: "In Chile, they apply the economic principles of the Chicago School. The same is done in the military dictatorships of Argentina and Uruguay ... Most of that money is stolen and leaves the country ... They loan us money at a low interest rate, and now collect it at a higher interest rate, with an overvalued dollar. Is it fair and is it legal, this policy: overvaluing the dollar, massive interest rates, unjust trade, the promoting and supporting of repressive and bloody governments, prescribing monetarist solutions to these same countries, and loaning them fantastic sums of money without considering how they will use it? Can this be justified, morally? ... Our conclusion is that we must resolve the problem of debt, or no democratic process will come together, and a social disaster will happen" (Interview with the Mexican newspaper *Excelsior*, March 21, 1985).

Starting over

In 1986, against an international background in which neoliberal ideology—which is both economic and military—begins to burn within the Soviet Union, Fidel Castro warns that if Cuba continues to import Soviet methods of social organization, it will run into serious danger in its confrontation with the US. Improving on the famous "perestroika" launched by the Soviet leader Mikhail Gorbachev, Fidel promotes the "Process of Rectification of Errors and Negative Tendencies" in Cuba.

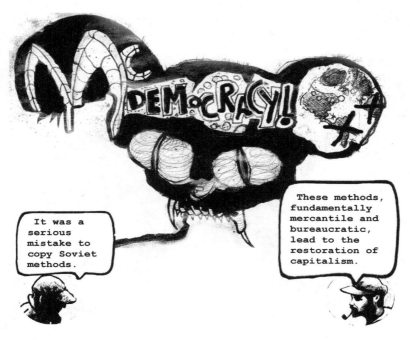

It was a serious mistake to copy Soviet methods.

These methods, fundamentally mercantile and bureaucratic, lead to the restoration of capitalism.

If, in the USSR, Gorbachev's "perestroika" criticizes Stalinism from the right (equating the market with democracy, and praising the "understanding" with Reagan and North American conservatives), in Cuba, Fidel's initiative questions Stalinism from the left, identifying the market with bureaucracy and socialism with anti-imperialism. It is no accident that during this process—in which Fidel revises not only the "*quinquenio gris*" of 1971–1976, but also the fifteen years in which pro-Soviet ideology was dominant in Cuba—Fidel comes to insist on a return to the revolutionary Marxism of Che Guevara.

We must return to Che!

In the middle of the final crisis of so-called "real socialism" in Eastern Europe, Fidel calls for a return to the study of Che. Paying homage to the twenty years since his murder, Fidel reflects: "Could there be a more opportune moment to remember Che than this, in the middle of our process of rectification? We are rectifying all the things that separated us from the revolutionary spirit, from revolutionary creativity, from revolutionary virtue, from revolutionary strength, from revolutionary responsibility, from the spirit of solidarity among men. We are rectifying every kind of bungling and mediocrity, which are the opposite of Che's ideas, of Che's revolutionary thinking, of Che's style, of Che's spirit, and of Che's example" (Speech of October 8, 1987).

Che was right! It's important to study his thought, not just to create a cult in his image. Che Guevara was an extraordinary fighter but also a magnificent Marxist thinker.

Fidel continues: "If Che were sitting here, he would be overjoyed and delighted with what we are doing; how disgraced he would have felt by that stifling period in which a series of opinions, bureaucratic mechanisms, and vices began to take control of the building of socialism; how that would have caused a deep, bitter sorrow in Che. What I ask modestly, on this twentieth anniversary, is that Che's economic ideas be known here, in Latin America, in the developed capitalist world, in the Third World, in the world of socialism—even *there* they should be known! They should be known!" (Speech of October 8, 1987).

Ethics and internationalism vs. the market

At the end of the 1980s, at the height of neoliberal counterrevolution around the world, a monetarist ideology begins to gain ground in the USSR and its allies. Abandoning what little Marxism they have left, the Soviet bureaucracy builds altars to the market. In Cuba, some groups feel attracted by this message. Applying the communist example of Che Guevara, Fidel argues against this version of socialism, which is on the verge of being neoliberalism. He insists, yet again, on the importance of values and socialist ethics in the face of the growing power of the market. This is a constant, one he repeats from the earliest formulations of his ideology until well into maturity.

We must make the economy efficient. Every business must make $$$. Those which can't make $$$ will have to close. We must adapt to the market.

No! Our strength is in ethics and values. We've fought with success against imperialism since our socialist culture began. It's not important that education and health don't make money for us. They'll continue to be free for all people!

Just as the USSR is feeling its death throes, in December 1989 the Cuban revolution pays tribute, through a symbolic funeral, to all of the Cuban internationalists, both civilian and military, who died fighting in other countries of the world, especially in Africa. The act is presided over by Fidel Castro and José Eduardo dos Santos, the president of Angola. Facing the dying world of Eastern Europe, Cuba still holds the flag of internationalism high.

The Soviet bureaucracy's moral crisis

From the 1930s—when, after Lenin's death, Stalinism consolidates its power—to 1989, many projects, speeches, ideologies, and leadership groups follow, one after the other, in the Soviet Union. Slowly, the great power begins to "adapt" to the established order. Long after its heroic people, in spite of Stalin's errors, defeated the ferocious genocide of the Nazis at a cost of twenty million lives, long after Stalin, Khrushchev, Brezhnev, and Gorbachev, the Soviet Union ends by giving Cuba a warning: if the US attacks, the USSR will not intercede.

Gorbachev

I'm sorry, comrade, but we can't help you against a military invasion by the US. You're completely alone.

We suspected that... it's incredible how pragmatism and "realism" always end up betraying the principles of revolution and internationalism.

This final abandonment of the minimum standards of internationalism toward Cuba goes hand in hand with the complete moral disarmament and putrefaction of the Soviet bureaucracy, now much more interested in securing its own economic future in the imminent restoration of capitalism—and in the privatization of the gigantic country—than in fighting for the ideals of socialism.

Fall of the Berlin Wall and the "special period"

In the 1950s, after the death of Stalin, the Soviet bureaucracy promotes "peaceful coexistence" with imperialism and begins to open progressively to the market. From this openness of the 1950s and 1960s to the stagnation of the 1970s and 1980s, and from there to the humiliating surrender, without honor, dignity, or glory, to world capitalism: in 1991 this same bureaucracy, corrupt and cruelly repressive, dissolves the USSR and becomes a brutal capitalist mafia.

With the fall of the Berlin Wall and the destruction of the USSR, the small Cuban revolution is left alone against the gigantic runaway world power, the United States. In the face of the collapse of Eastern Europe, Cuba loses 80 percent of its markets. Its foreign trade is quickly ruined. Fidel declares the 1990s to be a "special period," during which the continuity of the revolution runs its greatest risk. In this economic context, Cuba opens partially to the market and to foreign investments, albeit ones controlled by the state. This is not a new economic strategy, but a strict question of necessity, and survival at a critical time. Meanwhile, drunk with euphoria, the ideologues of the North American State Department proclaim: "The end of history!" (the title of a famous essay by Yankee philosopher and economist Francis Fukuyama).

The "special period" and poverty

After the fall of the Soviet Union, eighty percent of Cuban foreign trade collapses. Thus begins on the island a period of material need unknown in the history of the revolution. Fidel calls this the beginning of the "special period." The material poverty is also a result of the US political and economic blockade, by now a matter of tradition, which prohibits any company in the world from trading with the island or giving it credit, which creates major difficulties for the Cuban civilian population.

Despite the poverty and the economic crisis, neither medicine, food, nor books are denied to a single Cuban. During these difficult years, no one has expensive cars, fancy stereos, or DVD players, but despite this, the revolution has never privatized medical services or education. In the last few years, Cuba has left poverty behind, the economy has grown, and Cuba has received help from the Bolívarian government of Venezuela, led by Hugo Chávez, who controls a vast quantity of petroleum.

Tourism and repercussions in Cuba

As a result of the sudden loss of foreign trade when the USSR disappears, and the decline in the price of raw materials from Third World countries (sugar most of all), the economic crisis of the 1990s leaves the political leadership of the revolution no choice but to call on foreign tourism in order to earn dollars to buy medicine and other goods on the international market (the North American blockade requires Cuba to pay up front and in cash, since no one can extend credit to Cuba). Tourism has made a difference, but has had negative consequences on the socialist conscience of the young.

There are many kinds of foreign tourism in Cuba. An important group of tourists visits the island to get to know the culture and its advances in education, the arts, and society. Thousands and thousands of teachers, doctors, and economists from around the world come to attend the large conferences organized by Cuba, including the conferences on pedagogy and on globalization. But there is another group of tourists that comes with great buying power and with little interest in culture. They create within the minds of the Cuban people the false image that in all capitalist countries, everyone lives like a millionaire tourist (bogus images, in the light of day). Fidel Castro himself has warned against the negative influence of tourism and the market economy on the socialist conscience of the Cuban population, particularly on the young.

179

The North American blockade

The United States blockade against Cuba has continued for nearly fifty years. In February of 1962, the United States declares the beginning of an economic, financial, and commercial blockade against the island. From that moment until today, it has not ceased, even though it has been condemned many times by the United Nations.

The blockade obliges Cuba to always trade at a disadvantage, paying much higher prices than the market dictates, and trading only with those countries willing to defy the United States' government. Even many North American businesses, capitalists, and enemies of socialism are fed up with the Cuban blockade, because it stops them from making money and puts them at a disadvantage when competing with European companies.

What would have happened to any other Third World country that had to suffer a similar blockade for half a century? Could they have endured it? The revolution's ability to survive politically, despite its being subjected to a blockade: isn't that because of the great affinity between Fidel and the people?

Free and social medicine

In Cuba, health care is completely free, and every family has its own primary care physician. But this standard of medical care, famous around the world due to its positive evaluations from the Pan-American Health Organization and the World Health Organization, is not limited to the island. The International Cuban Health Cooperation began in Africa in 1963 with aid given to Algeria. From 1963 until today, thirty-eight thousand Cuban doctors have dispensed free aid in ninety-two countries, mainly in the Third World. In addition, more than two thousand foreign doctors have studied for free in Cuba, and Cuban teachers have organized eight medical facilities, mostly in African countries, where they have trained hundreds of doctors.

He is Hatian, I am from Bolivia. We are studying medicine for free in Cuba so we can return to our countries and help the poor.

In 1998, Fidel Castro opens the Latin American Medical School, completely free, which has fifteen thousand students per year (from twenty-four countries, nineteen of them Latin American, four from Africa, and the rest of the students from the US). The first class graduates in 2005. While the Pentagon exports war and marines wherever it wants, Cuba exports doctors to the poorest and neediest corners of the world.

Cuba exports the most dangerous weapon of all...

Defying the massive anti-Cuba campaigns by United States press agencies, Fidel Castro's government has taken charge of exporting the "explosive weapon" that has been so successful in dealing with Cuban internal affairs: literacy. The new program begins as a test in Haiti in 2002, with classes broadcast by radio. Little by little, they improve the teaching system until it is upgraded to an audiovisual system, as is used today. The project, which uses educational videos and television to teach reading, is called *Yo, sí puedo* (*Yes, I Can*) and is created by the Latin American and Caribbean Institute of Pedagogy in Cuba.

The very powerful are frightened of the "Cuban weapons exportation" program. But the most dangerous weapons Cuba exports are its tools for teaching people to read...

From Cuba, the literacy method is "exported" to Argentina in 2003, to Mexico, to Hugo Chávez's Venezuela—a country declared free of illiteracy and held up as an example—to Bolivia, to Ecuador, and to Paraguay, where teachers are now adapting it to use for the indigenous language Guaraní. The method has also been used outside of Latin America by the people of New Zealand, who call the program *Green Life*, and by teachers in Africa. The program targets people fifteen years old and older, and teaches reading and writing using educational videos—each video made up of seventeen short films—in which a virtual teacher invites the students to take the first steps toward learning. In addition, the program uses primers, which the IPLAC sends to each country, that contain the alphabet, numbers, and many essays designed to make learning and studying easier.

Fidel vs. defeatism

In the 1950s, some defeatist speakers, supposedly "orthodox" and "scientific," argued that since Cuba had underdeveloped forces of production, a radical social revolution was not viable. Later, in the 1960s, these same speakers—critics of Che and Fidel—argued that that Cuba was not "mature enough" for socialism. Much later, in the 1990s, these same speakers assert that (a) the USSR fell, not because of bureaucracy, but because of "underdeveloped forces of production," and (b) there is no sense in Cuba continuing to resist, since its economy is very weak, and since it has not developed its forces of production…

In the 1990s, just as in the 1950s and 1960s, Fidel Castro argues venomously against this defeatism. Revolution, socialism, and resistance are entirely possible, realistic, and viable. The key to resistance, and to the refusal of total surrender—even without trade from the USSR, without oil, and without wealth—is in the subjectivity of the people, in the creation of the "new man" and the "new woman," in the new culture, and in the values of solidarity, the self-esteem of the people, patriotism, anti-imperialism, and socialist ethics.

Chávez and Fidel

Even though the Sandinista revolution, a long-time ally of Cuba, is defeated in the elections of 1990 and Granada is invaded by the US, Fidel gains a new and unexpected Latin American ally against the North American superpower. He meets with Hugo Chávez, an anti-imperialist and a follower of Bolívar. He is a military man *sui generis* who reads Eduardo Galeano and can quote readily from Antonio Gramsci, Leon Trotsky, Rosa Luxembourg, and Che Guevara. Chávez becomes a close friend of Fidel, to the point that he publicly declares: "Fidel is like a father to me."

The sword of Bolívar returns. Imperialism trembles. The future belongs to us: Latin America, united and socialist!

Just as it was during the first phase of the Cuban revolution or the Sandinista revolution, the United States violently opposes the Bolívarist process in Venezuela. On April 11, 2002, the Venezuelan military stages a coup d'état against Chávez. According to the book *El código Chávez: Descifrando la intervención de los EEUU en Venezuela* (Buenos Aires: Question, 2005), written by the US intellectual Eva Golinger, the CIA, by means of the group known as the National Endowment for Democracy (NED), is in direct contact with the planners of the coup, encouraging their actions and financing their plans. But the coup fails spectacularly due to the overwhelming support for Venezuela's democratically-elected president. At the moment of the coup, on the phone, Fidel urges Chávez not to follow Allende's path by killing himself. Today, defying the US, Chávez pursues what he calls "socialism for the twenty-first century."

Cuba and the United States

While the North American extreme right prohibits US citizens from visiting Cuba, having any cultural exchange, or even being tourists on the island (if a citizen disobeys, he or she is severely punished), the political leadership of the revolution is intent on breaking the Yankee blockade. For this reason, they invite many priests, filmmakers, social militants, and even former US President Jimmy Carter, who visits Cuba in 2002. Carter speaks in public on Cuban television from the University of Havana.

As we have invited you, Mr. President, we invite any North American president to come to Cuba and publicly debate about capitalism and socialism.

Trying to dispel the Cold War image that the United States press has created about Cuba and the socialist revolution, Fidel notes about former President Jimmy Carter's visit to the island: "The Cuban people have a political culture; they are not fanatics. One can remain strong forever to the extent that it sustains one's own ideas and convictions, not by fanaticism. The Cuban revolution never blamed the North American people, even though a majority of North American citizens are persuaded by everything that has been said about Cuba, that we are a threat to US security. Cuba welcomes North Americans with respect, and without being offended at all" (*Mi vida,* a biography/interview with Ignacio Ramonet).

Rebellion and resistance to globalization

Although Fukuyama's capitalist euphoria and the arrogance of North American imperialism promise that the US and the neoliberals will rule for a thousand years—the dream of Hitler—neoliberalism quickly enters a crisis. As they learn about old errors and defeats, the resistance continues and new rebellions appear. Even in the middle of the worst neoliberal aggression, the Cuban revolution continues to be attractive.

Che lives and Fidel is our teacher.
The resistance grows.
The future is socialism.

If, in the 1990s, Fidel and the Cuban revolution found themselves alone against a runaway giant, at the beginning of the twenty-first century the situation is different. On a worldwide scale, a movement critical of global capitalism has begun. In every city and nation, a new organization of those who oppose the systematic injustices of capitalism and imperialism is emerging. In other words: these new social movements are reclaiming the internationalist spirit that the Cuban revolution promotes. From Cuba, Fidel holds many events designed to help initiate, organize, and coordinate these worldwide protests, from annual forums on pedagogy and on the fight against globalization to the organization of "Intellectuals and Artists in Defense of Humanity."

Socialism versus the capitalist anti-utopia

Just as the internal politics of the United States become worse—McCarthyism, the absolute monopoly of the media, the surveillance of citizens, the opening of private mail, wiretapping, recording of all emails and library books, and the conversion of any average citizen into a "suspect"—from outside US borders, barefaced US interventionism by the Yankee military and NATO is becoming stronger. In the name of "globalization," it all multiplies: wars for oil, military bases, concentration camps, and torture in many countries.

Abu Ghraib Prison - Iraq

29 5 2006

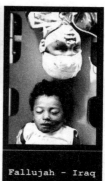

Fallujah - Iraq

Enough with torture and
concentration camps; enough with
wars for money and oil!
Enough with hunger and exploitation!
We struggle together, all of us, and
all of us against imperialism!

And facing this somber capitalist anti-utopia of our times, against which Huxley's *Brave New World*, Bradbury's *Fahrenheit 451*, and Orwell's *1984* all pale: At the beginning of the twenty-first century, Fidel Castro puts forth the call for a worldwide struggle against neoliberalism, and against the wars and the neofascist goals of contemporary imperialism.

Fidel: both of us dedicated our lives to revolution and socialism. How do you see the future?

Calmly, and with much hope! I feel the same faith and enthusiasm as I did when we met each other. We planted the seed. Whether our ideals will bloom is in the hands of the young.

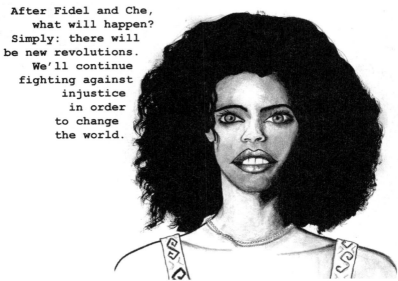

After Fidel and Che, what will happen? Simply: there will be new revolutions. We'll continue fighting against injustice in order to change the world.

Epilogue

In 2006, following a severe illness, Fidel Castro transferred his responsibilities as president to his brother Raúl Castro. Although he recovered, on February 18, 2008, Fidel officially resigned as the president and commander in chief of Cuba. Six days later, Raúl Castro was officially sworn in as president by a unanimous vote of the Cuban National Assembly.

Despite no longer being the functional head of the revolution, Fidel is still consulted on vital matters of the Cuban government, and remains the First Secretary of the Cuban Communist Party. In addition, his example and his internationalist beliefs continue to inspire anti-imperialist revolutions around the world: In September 2009, the United Nations General Assembly named him a "World Hero of Solidarity." He continues to write his thoughts on world politics on his blog, "Reflections of the Commander in Chief" (http://www.cuba.cu/gobierno/reflexiones/reflexiones.html).

About the Author

NÉSTOR KOHAN (Buenos Aires, 1967) is a teacher and researcher at the University of Buenos Aires. Inspired by Marxism, he has discovered a simple and inexpensive therapy for the stresses of modern life, one which consists simply of never bowing and scraping to anyone and never taking any shit. For practicing this therapy, he has been fired from many organizations and lost several jobs. He is the author of *Gramsci for Beginners, Marxism for Beginners, Marx in His (Third) World, From Ingenieros to Che: Essays About Argentinean and Latin American Marxism, Ernesto Che Guevara: The Individual and the Force, Toni Negri and the Challenges of Empire, Das Kapital: History and Method, Deodoro Roca the Heretic, The Armor-Plated Rose: A Passion from the 1960s,* and many more. He is a follower of Marx, Lukács, Rosa Luxembourg, Lenin, Gramsci, Adolfo Sánchez Vásquez, Carlos Tablada, and Armando Hart Dávalos. Reclaiming the forgotten heritage of Paul Lafargue, he aspires to one day write *How to Live Without Working For Beginners,* but for now he can find no solution to the problem.

About the Illustrator

NAHUEL SCHERMA (Buenos Aires, 1976) is an expert in ad design, a job that in Argentina certifies him as "creative." He studied audiovisual production in the National University of La Plata and also studied film editing at the National School for Cinematographic Experimentation and Production. Since the year 2000, he has been a member of the group *Cine insurgente.* There, he and others collectively produced many documentaries, and he teaches documentary production in the communications department of the People's University Madres de Plaza de Mayo, where he is also a founding member of the video library. He has worked as a photographer, cameraman, editor, storyboard artist, and slave on many prestigious productions. In 2005, he produced the short film *Abril primera parte (The First Part of April),* which was shown in more than thirty festivals and conferences both in Argentina and abroad. *Fidel* is his first book of drawings.

About Seven Stories Press

Seven Stories Press is an independent book publisher based in New York City, with distribution throughout the United States, Canada, England, and Australia. We publish works of the imagination by such writers as Nelson Algren, Russell Banks, Octavia E. Butler, Ani DiFranco, Assia Djebar, Ariel Dorfman, Coco Fusco, Barry Gifford, Hwang Sokyong, Lee Stringer, and Kurt Vonnegut, to name a few, together with political titles by voices of conscience, including the Boston Women's Health Collective, Noam Chomsky, Angela Y. Davis, Human Rights Watch, Derrick Jensen, Ralph Nader, Gary Null, Project Censored, Barbara Seaman, Gary Webb, and Howard Zinn, among many others. Seven Stories Press believes publishers have a special responsibility to defend free speech and human rights, and to celebrate the gifts of the human imagination, wherever we can. For additional information, visit www.sevenstories.com.